EXCEPTIONAL
SERVICE
MAKES SENSE...
BUSINESS SENSE

SALLY PRESCOTT

WHAT PEOPLE ARE SAYING ABOUT
Exceptional Service Makes Sense

———

'An honest and refreshing approach in making a positive difference to your business through excellent customer service. Sally demystifies the essence of what great customer service looks like through real life scenarios and practical exercises — definitely a book to keep and refer back to.

Sally's hospitality experience combined with her passion for world class, authentic customer service really shines through in this inspiring and informative book that provides a clear step-by-step guide to anyone from the person starting out in business to the senior business leader.

I would never have thought the five senses of see, hear, smell, taste and feel could be used as a framework for delivering excellent service but it actually makes perfect sense — a practical and creative book to help us all challenge the way we deliver customer service.'

Clive Doble, Tourism Director,
Value Retail Management (Bicester Village) Ltd

'A wonderful read! Learning how to build confidence in delivering service excellence is the key to success and Sally has shared her expertise in helping you do just this. She shows us how building emotional connections drives customer loyalty and future returns.'

Eugenio Pirri, Chief People & Culture Officer,
Global Diversity Champion, Dorchester Collection

'A MUST READ to any business owner or senior manager who has a customer-facing business! This is not just a reading book...Sally makes you dig deep into your mind and really consider how you (& your team) can make your business offer truly exceptional service. I have no doubt anyone working through this book will gain fantastic business results as we plan to do!'

Heather Hiley, Ecommerce Business Owner

'This down-to-earth guide to achieving exceptional service is thoughtfully laid out with practical exercises that really make the reader think. Sally really knows her craft from her own practical experience. In this excellent book she generously shares her skills, knowledge and techniques - definitely worth a read.'

Jane Sunley, CEO, Purple Cubed

'This book makes for an exciting read; practical and common sense with a major emphasis on helping any organisation deliver exceptional service.

Customer is key and without customers any business is worthless.

This honest and passionate way to achieve the exceptional in everything you do is a must read which can work in any organisation and culture.

Having worked with Sally closely she massively changed our learning style and helped us to improve our customer and colleague satisfaction, enabling us to deliver the exceptional service expected from our customers. Would highly recommend this book to any organisation.'

Katherine Bent, Head of People and Culture,
Bents Garden and Home

'I found it "exceptional". It is, without doubt, one of the most comprehensive expositions on the subject of customer service I have seen. It delves into the key issues in detail whilst at all times remaining light and accessible. That's quite some feat! I particularly like the use of anecdotes which help steer the narrative away from the 'preachy' style I have seen in so many other publications on the subject.'

James Berresford, Board Member,
Peak District National Park

'This book is a must for anyone who is starting their career or for someone who is a seasoned professional. With easy-to-understand language and real-life examples, Sally truly gives you the insider information, advice and guidance. Use this as your bible if you care about exceptional service and it will make sense.'

Sam Coulstock FIH MIEP, CEO & Founder,
INSPIRED Community Group CIC

'Generous and inspired! At long last we finally have a book about exceptional service that really does *make sense*. The author's generosity in sharing an abundance of practical tips and activities challenges us to take a fresh and honest look at our service provision. A must read for any business owner and manager who wishes to improve their customer service or dares to think they already have it covered!'

Gary Churton, Leadership Team Coach and Group Facilitator,
MD Tailored Development

'As the Hospitality Industry comes to terms with the challenges Brexit, Covid 19, global travel and climate change forces up on us, there is a nervousness and lack of confidence, not only from bosses and their teams, but customers alike, so effectively re engaging with your customers is now more important than ever.

This need not be an arduous ask, as Sally says in her practical and refreshingly energetic new book, *Exceptional Service Makes Sense*, 'Sometimes it just takes a fresh pair of eyes and a new approach'.

This book is a very usable resource in your journey to start rebuilding your team's self-belief in delivering exceptional service consistently in these demanding times.'

Richard J Murcott FIH, former Hotelier & Company Director

Exceptional Service Makes Sense
By Sally Prescott
ISBN: 978-1-8384363-0-8
Copyright © 2021 Sally Prescott

Copyeditor and proofreader: Siân-Elin Flint-Freel
Book design by Tanya Back, www.tanyabackdesigns.com

CHAPTERS
AND APPENDICES

Who Is Your Customer? 23

What Our Customers Want To See 29

What Our Customers Want To Hear 49

What Our Customers Want To Smell 73

What Our Customers Want To Taste 85

What We Want Our Customers To Feel 101

What We Want Our Customers To Feel...
Emotionally Connected 115

6 Steps To Exceptional Service 131

What If... It Doesn't Go As We Intended? 167

Be Exceptional 191

Leading 207

Enjoy Every Moment 211

Appendix A 215

Appendix B 226

Appendix C 228

PROLOGUE

No matter what your business is or what you do, you have customers. Customer service and an excellent customer experience is critical to the future of your business. When you get this right, it is more likely that your customers will return and even recommend your services to others. An exceptional reputation as an individual, team or business leads to expansion opportunities with positive benefits for everyone. The aim of this book is to take an honest look at your business and to use that new perspective to create exceptional service. It is practical, doable and will make a positive difference.

As you read this book, I'm sure that there will be times when you will think that it is simple, basic or even believe that you already do it all. However, to put some of the basics in place and to get the customer experience right is hard work. We like to think that we do it all the time. I can honestly say we don't. We often get it wrong. As soon as we accept that we all sit in the biggest room in the universe— 'the room for improvement'—that's when things will progress. We put our ego to one side and search for ways to become even better.

I invite you to challenge yourself, to take a step back and consider your business. See the experience from the customer's point of view, or even ask one or two of them. Ask yourself: 'Do we deliver what we say we will?' and 'What can we do to be even better?'

We often forget what we're striving to achieve in our own business, we make assumptions as things seem obvious to us; however, these things may not be so obvious to our customers or our teams. This book encourages you to take a step or two in the shoes of your customers and experience your business from their perspective, so you can show your team what an exceptional experience would look and feel like. This will enable your team to be clear about what is expected and feel confident in their delivery.

In order to do this, you need to satisfy your customers' five senses so that doing business with you is a pleasure. The ultimate aim is to create an emotional exceptional experience for all your customers, to win their hearts and minds.

Make your business the obvious choice in your industry.

If you get the basics right for each individual customer and they receive the attention that they need, their requirements are heard and fulfilled, they **feel** valued and the whole experience causes them to **feel** that their experience was great value for money, then they are likely to remember you and return.

So, join me in considering each step of your customer's interaction with you and your business which contributes to their service experience. Step inside.

INTRODUCTION

Are you a business owner who wants to improve the results within your business? Do you want to be renowned as exceptional within your industry? Would you like to improve the customer experience throughout your business? You are probably working with customers on a daily basis and can see opportunities to improve the experience you offer to them. Is the product and service you offer aligned to what your customers want? Are you proud of the products and service experience all your customers receive?

Customer service is crucial in creating the experience that leads to client loyalty and is vital to the success of any business, especially in the hospitality industry. However, this is also the case in all businesses where a customer is present—**all** businesses.

My passion for people and service began when I was very young. My parents owned a newsagent and we lived in the flat above the business from when I was 18 months to 12 years old.

I enjoyed being in the shop with the regular customers. As soon as I was old enough, I'd help in the shop and learned some fundamental principles. Mum used to correct my enthusiastic re-stocking of the chocolate bars, ensuring that all the existing stock was brought to the front with the new stock at the back, and checking that all the product labels were facing forward and the right way up. This valuable lesson of ensuring good stock rotation as well as making sure that the display looked appealing and well presented, neat and tidy, was drummed into me from an early age and proved invaluable later in life.

Something that stood out for me was the community spirit that existed in the shop; the regular customers would stand around and have a good chat, with many bouts of laughter and great fun. Ten o'clock in the morning was 'coffee time'. Mum or Dad would make coffee for themselves and Francis, our shop assistant, which would mean three mugs of coffee on a tray. However, the number of mugs would often be six, seven or eight as they'd make a coffee for the regular customers too. Ten o'clock in the shop was busy! I'm sure if they had their newsagents today, it would have a coffee shop element to it. (Actually, probably not the best idea as they'd be giving the coffee away!)

Skipping a number of years, I chose a career in hospitality, which I still love. I could start promoting all the great reasons why a career in hospitality is so amazing. However, that would take me totally off track. Oh go on then, I can't resist. Here are just a few great reasons: it gave me the opportunity to meet a variety of people from different backgrounds and cultures, whether working with them or looking after them. It offered many opportunities for overseas experience to learn and understand so much about diverse working and living. Working in hospitality is often perceived to be the typical roles of waiter, chef or receptionist, but it led to me gaining a degree and having a career shift that gave me the required experience to further my career in any industry. I'd do it all over again—although with the lessons I have now learned, of course.

Having progressed my career from being a receptionist to leading teams in five-star hotels, it taught me what is critical to the success of a business:

Look after the people in your organisation and they will look after your customers and business.

Success happens when the team is happy, and when they are clear about what is important. Looking after customers or guests is fundamental to business success, and when all team members know and work towards ensuring this, that is when the magic happens.

During my career, I have learned so much, and I continue to do so. I know at times I have cut corners on things that I thought didn't matter so much. For example, it didn't matter if the carpet wasn't immaculately vacuumed ready for a conference party's arrival. After all, the room would soon be full of people, so who would notice? Now I realise that *I* would (and *do*) spot these things, therefore there will be other people who notice too.

As a leader in the three-star hotel market, I was quite naïve at times when I visited the competition. It's important to keep an eye on what's going on with competitors and I would ensure that I made regular visits. However, when I look back, I would often have a mindset of 'That would never happen in my hotel!' I'd take joy in believing the service or product we were offering was superior and would only concentrate on that, giving me a sense of complacency. What I have come to understand is that visiting other hotels gives me the ideal opportunity to learn what they do well. What do they do that impresses me? How can we do what they do and potentially build on it to be even better?

How can I upgrade our product or service to be even better?

The reality was that my team wasn't perfect (I don't know any team that is). As a team, there were times when we didn't prepare as well as we could have. We lacked the foresight of effective communication. It's hard to take a look at yourself and challenge the way you do things. More importantly, the more senior we become as we build on our careers, the trickier it is to know what is going on with each interaction with our customers. We think our teams are performing the service and products as we have it in our heads. The ultimate question is, are they?

My next career move took me to a five-star hotel, and what stood out for me was the amount of pride that oozed from the team who worked there. Detail really does matter. There was a huge amount of precise preparation, consideration and thought that went into making the guest/customer experience exceptional.

I also learned that the five-star world is daunting for many people. Inducting our new colleagues into the world of five star and their new roles was an important part of the experience we wanted for our team. We'd dine in one of the hotel restaurants, so they gained an understanding of what it is like to be a guest. On one occasion, a colleague (who was due to work in one of our restaurants) quietly asked me which cutlery to use to eat their meal. This showed me how important it is to guide the team in fully understanding what the business is striving to achieve, and more importantly, for colleagues to feel confident. We need to help the teams within our organisations to be clear about the service we expect for our customers.

My last employed role was in a five-star hotel that was serious about service, their team and about converting profit—and it did. This was not easy to do, that's for sure, yet everyone knew what they had to do, felt valued and were committed to delivering exceptional results—most of the time!

The **huge** lesson learned is that it doesn't matter what star rating or what style of product or level of service you are offering, all customers can have a five-star experience. Being 'serious' about service is the ultimate key to success; this needs to run through every single member of your team. It's all about being proud of your product. It being presented in the best possible way. Are you and your team presented in the best possible way? Does the service your customers experience leave them feeling valued and wanting to return?

As well as being passionately interested in customer service, another reason to write this book is the huge amount of experience I have as a customer, as I'm sure you have too. You can go to the corner shop and have a five-star experience, where the store is immaculate, well presented, you feel welcomed, valued and leave with exactly what you want and maybe more, with a smile on your face. When you have these kinds of experiences you don't even think about how much money you've spent. On the other hand, in some exclusive shops, restaurants, hotels, or professional services, you are frequently ignored or you're directed to someone else by a person whose attention you've managed to get but seems not to be bothered. These organisations are charging premium prices and this is simply rude. It reminds me of the scene in the film *Pretty Woman* where the shop assistants refuse to assist Julia Roberts, and as she says when she returns, 'Big mistake, huge!'

When a celebrity walks into these fancy establishments, they gain all the attention. I always wonder how many celebrities visit the establishment versus other customers. Lesson One: there is more opportunity to build customer loyalty through normal (whatever normal is) customers than celebrities. You can continue to look after these high-profile people as you do. However, treat all the other people in the same way, if not even better. This is how customers become super loyal to your business. I realise that people or organisations will suck up to the people with an abundance of money. This makes sense. However, I've yet to establish what a millionaire looks like! My conclusion is that they look like a human. We have no idea of the status of their bank balance, so why don't we look after all customers? Each person has the ability to talk about his or her experience. You decide what you'd like them to say by how you treat them.

As I have said, in every business there is a customer. Yet, some of these businesses can become a little complacent about this. They lose focus and forget to listen and respond to their most treasured person in their business—the customer.

If you're not looking after a customer directly, you are most probably supporting a colleague who is. For example, a waiter is serving a paying customer; the chef may not be in direct contact with the customer but supports the waiter. In fact, the waiter is the chef's internal customer. Therefore, the manner in which the chef communicates with the waiter is just as important because this leads to the way the waiter communicates with the paying customer. Taking this example a step further, if the waiter has been given feedback by a customer, they need to feel secure that they can share this with the chef, knowing they will be listened to and an adequate response will be given.

This is also the case for most back-office functions, such as finance and HR. Each role is contributing in some way to the customer experience. It is an exceptional experience when the request being made on behalf of the customer is heard and responded to with a generous spirit, helpfulness and flexibility to assist the front-facing member of staff (the waiter in the previous example) and their customer.

Rather than putting the customer first, what seems to happen is that customers are processed in a certain way so it is easier for us, the supplier or provider of the services. This happens frequently with accountants, solicitors, banks, builders, plumbers, electricians and medical professionals.

I see and hear of so many businesses monitoring their financial results, spending so much time examining each entry line by line, looking at ways to possibly save money or increase their profitable results. I appreciate that senior roles will of course need to examine their accounts to consider future investments, etc. Yet the best thing they can do to influence their finances is to ensure that each customer receives exactly what they want in a way that leaves them feeling valued, appreciated and considered. Spending more time influencing the care of the customer is far more productive and will lead to improved financial results. Yet I continue to see less time spent on placing the customer at the centre. I know this because of the way I feel so often as a customer.

Overall, wherever there is a customer, consider how you can improve the experience. That will satisfy the needs of your customer, which will then have a hugely positive impact on your profitability.

It's simple:

No customers = No business.

What type of experience do you want your customers to have?

The aim of this book is to encourage all service providers, middle managers, senior leaders and business owners to stop and re-consider what kind of service and experience your customers are currently having. And from this new understanding, to improve that experience and to get to a position where you can celebrate and feel proud of your business.

We have become detached from the front line of service and don't know what is happening with our customers. In my mind, what we need to do is to make it easy for our customers to spend money. It's not about being a great salesperson; it's about offering exceptional service. (We do need to sell too!)

It is *Zest for Life*'s ambition for the UK and beyond to be renowned for genuine service, where consumers feel valued. When customers feel this, they become loyal. This will, of course, have a positive impact on the economic performance of your business. You will find that this is mentioned a few times. It's a point that requires re-iterating, as it seems people forget.

To achieve this, everyone within the business needs to understand how important each and every interaction with the customer is, whether you are dealing with a customer directly or supporting someone else who is, or preparing the product for the customer's use. Each interaction is crucial to your business success. That is why I have developed the *Exceptional Service Makes Sense* method. The step-by-step process encourages you to become aware of the five senses of **See, Hear, Smell, Taste and Feel** as you walk through your business. This helps you to recognise where your business needs improvement.

You will then identify *10 priority service standards* that you'll observe in your business, which you assess each week. As these service standards become embedded and are removed from the list, you can add new standards to assess. Each time, your service standards will be improving, leading you towards service excellence.

Once you have these basic standards in place, you will then be able to move on to the *Zest for Life 6 Steps to Exceptional Service*. These create an emotional connection with the guest/customer, so your team considers the needs of each customer as an individual. The approach is to consider the 'one' customer who is using your business at that time, rather than giving the customer the impression of being processed along a conveyor belt and not having their individual needs considered in the process.

I'm encouraging you to take a closer look at your business from your customer's point of view. Ask yourself the question:

What do you want to be renowned for?
What legacy do you want leave?

Take this to the next level and consider what your customers want and need. Then deliver this continuously—this is where the magic really happens.

So, why is it so important to have the basics in place before you progress to connect emotionally with your customers? Because what the customer sees, hears, smells, tastes and feels has a massive impact. There are some organisations who interact with their customers on an exceptional level, yet their premises are dirty and uninviting. This then cancels the fabulous interactions the customer may have experienced. A whole pile of effort is lost as a result of the basics not being in place.

By following the process, you will be able to take your business from where it is today to an exceptional level, where you feel confident and proud of every interaction your customers have with the people in your team. Your team will pro-actively seek feedback and feel confident in responding appropriately.

This book will assist you to re-focus and to take steps to improve. If you are a middle manager or leader, you may want to assess the service performance of your team privately initially, then share with them what you are striving to achieve and involve them in their assessment criteria so they own their own targets. You may even want to create a scoreboard to get the team focused and energised on having a positive impact on the results, considering areas for improvement, noticing who and what the team do well and then challenge yourselves to become even better.

If you are a senior leader or business owner, this book will assist you in refocusing on the core of what your business is all about—your customer. Whilst you are building the 3-5 or 5-10 year strategy, it is crucial that you are proud of the service your customers receive today, so you can be confident that you have a business to consider in the future! Complacency is the reason for so many businesses failing. You may want daily updates on the service levels of your organisation. Place these alongside your financial results to get a true holistic picture of how your teams are performing.

Throughout this book you will be asked some questions regarding your own business. Take time to think about your responses as they will help you discover what you are striving to achieve and how to achieve it.

Here's an exercise to get you started:

INTENTION, BEHAVIOUR AND IMPACT

When you arrive at work each day, what is your intention? That may seem like a difficult question to answer. At the beginning of my career, I would probably have shrugged my shoulders and said, "To do a good job." That's all well and good, but how would other people be able to interpret that "doing a good job" is my intention through the way I behave?

To tease this out a little further, take a look at the following statements and tick the top three which best describe your intention at work.

- [ ] To go through the pain and get out of here
- [ ] To sell as much as I can
- [ ] To win
- [ ] To have fun
- [ ] To make the business more profitable
- [ ] To maintain and build on the great reputation of the business
- [ ] To avoid annoying customers or colleagues
- [ ] To gain recognition and get promoted
- [ ] To fulfill my role in maintaining the correct standards
- [ ] To enjoy the social aspects of being at work
- [ ] To support my colleagues
- [ ] To deliver amazing service for our customers
- [ ] To meet the customers' needs
- [ ] Something else? Specify here:

So, if you were to have an out-of-body experience and could witness how you are at work, does your behaviour match your intention?

To help you answer this, select your three most common behaviours at work.

- [ ] Efficient
- [ ] Rushed and focused on tasks
- [ ] Listening carefully to customers
- [ ] Stressed under pressure
- [ ] Blame others

- [ ] With empathy
- [ ] Joking around
- [ ] Quiet and shy
- [ ] Supportive
- [ ] Moaning about others to colleagues
- [ ] Friendly and approachable
- [ ] Abrupt
- [ ] Calm under pressure
- [ ] Miserable
- [ ] Bored
- [ ] Something else? Specify here:

From your 'out-of-body' vantage point, how do you think your behaviours impact on other people within the business, whether it be customers or colleagues?

If your intention is to do a good job, then your behaviour needs to reflect that intention.

Take a few moments to consider how your behaviours impact the customer and your colleagues. Which three would you say best describes the impact you have on others?

- [ ] Customers trust me and the business
- [ ] Customers like talking to me
- [ ] Customers feel that we're serious about good service and want to return
- [ ] Customers feel that I care
- [ ] Customers are willing to share their feedback with me
- [ ] Most customers seem unhappy with the service provided
- [ ] Customers are grateful for the service e.g. I get lots of tips
- [ ] Colleagues don't seem to want to socialise with me
- [ ] Colleagues are reluctant to ask for my advice
- [ ] Colleagues have fun when they work with me
- [ ] Colleagues appreciate my support
- [ ] Colleagues often question the way I do things
- [ ] Something else? Specify here:

Of course, the same goes for your colleagues and members of your team. Their behaviours have an impact on you, their colleagues and customers. Take a few moments to consider the people you work with and how their behaviour has an impact.

All I can say is, how you and your team behave has an impact. If your intention is not gaining the impact that you wish, then you need to make some alterations to your behaviour. If you want to make serious changes to gain a much-improved impact, take time to seriously consider what your intention is for each day, including every interaction and conversation with others. Behave in a way that will have the impact that you intend. Every interaction with a customer is having an impact. Are these interactions positive or not so? What behaviours might need adjusting?

Capture your thoughts here:

How to use this book

You will be taken on a customer journey of your organisation. This journey will enable you to walk in your customers' shoes and refresh your own view, which may have become a bit blinkered over time. In some ways, it is similar to when you want to sell your house; the experts come in and advise how to make your house 'sale ready'. They see things that you can no longer see. They consider the curb appeal, de-cluttering, creating the right aromas with coffee or bread, etc. They consider the sounds from the nearby road and strive to encourage viewing when the sounds aren't so obvious, maybe avoiding rush hour. The preparation is all built around the senses. Their overall aim is to build desire, to encourage a feeling of being connected to the house, creating a feeling of love and longing for more. Each of the senses connect to our thoughts and link to how we then feel.

In the same way, we shall build a sensory experience for your business, examining the senses one by one: sight, hearing, taste, smell and feeling. 'Feeling' is the last sensing chapter. However, this is the biggest to explore, with the potential to take your customer experience way beyond what they could potentially imagine.

Each chapter will encourage you to think like a customer within your business, and what the impact could be of neglecting any one of the senses when reviewing your customers' experiences.

In your business, some of the senses may not seem crucial. However, I'd suggest you give them due attention as you may be surprised in what you discover. For example, in professional offices such as a solicitor, you may have become 'nose-blind' to the strong bleach smell from the toilets, yet your customers detect it straight away.

Stories and real-life examples will demonstrate the value added by exceptional service. They will describe a customer journey within a range of businesses and can be related to all businesses. These examples will give you the opportunity to consider what could have been done differently. It will also give you the chance to take a serious look at your business and consider whether this could have been the case if it had happened to you or with your team. If so, what do you need to do to improve?

In my experience, we are our own greatest critics. If we can take an objective view of how we're doing, we give ourselves more and more opportunities to become even better. This will create a passion about service which is as important as the financial results.

Each chapter will give you the tools to identify and address any issues which could impact on your customer's experience. By following the steps, you will create your own self-assessment. This can be shared with your team, so that they are clear on what is expected.

There will be a *Service Standards Checklist* at the end of each chapter, which will enable you to evaluate your business. The sensory standards (based on see, hear, smell, taste and feel) ensure you have not overlooked the basic things. When you and your team have these in place, you can progress to the next level of service delivery. The list of standards will assist you. However, should you wish to adapt these so they are more relevant to your business, then go for it.

It will take time to shift from where you are now. Starting at the beginning is important; skipping to exceptional will mean that the vital foundational elements will be overlooked. Getting the basics right is crucial. Take the time to embed the good before you move on to becoming exceptional.

In Chapter 8 you will be guided through the *6 Steps to Exceptional Service*. It's all about making it special for each individual customer, where they leave the experience with your business wanting to tell others, the best kind of advertising you could possibly wish for. This is where we shift our focus to think about the 'one' customer rather than all of our customers. Are you aspiring to offer a good service where your customers get what they want and need? Would you prefer it to be great, where they leave thinking that was far better than they had expected? Or potentially, would you rather their experience is exceptional, where they feel valued, heard and considered? I'd imagine your response to this last question is a resounding 'Yes'!

There may be obstacles in the way, and there is also the issue of customer feedback. Customers have many opportunities to share the good and not so good experiences they've received via social media. It is important that we pay attention to these comments. However, these are subjective, based on their perspective. Chapter 9 will consider how to respond when the customer is not satisfied with the product or service they have received. There are ways to ensure that you and your team are confident and keen to find out about any of areas of dissatisfaction before your customers leave your business. Make it easy for your customer to share their point of view. By creating and embedding the *Service Standards Checklists*, you will have a clear perspective of your service delivery from an objective standpoint. This will enable a team culture of welcoming and responding appropriately to any feedback. With this approach, your customers are likely to make comments about how well you and your team respond to any niggles they might have, as well as the comments about your exceptional service.

Taking the lead in creating exceptional service requires each individual within the team to understand the important part they play. Chapters 10 and 11 are relevant even if you are not leading a team of people, but you are reading this book because you want to take ownership of your own delivery. Taking the lead in service will fill you with confidence when handling customers. You will see the difference in yourself. I also believe that others will notice too. Your customers will, for sure.

In summary, there are four stages covered in the book:
1. Getting the basics in place for 'all customers'.
2. Behaving in a way that emotionally connects with 'one customer' at one time.
3. Embracing feedback and being confident in your response when a customer is dis-satisfied.
4. Creating and embedding the Zest for Life method to constantly and consistently measure and improve your service delivery.

These four stages will lead to BE EXCEPTIONAL.

To get you started, take a few minutes to think of 10 things you want your customers to experience. This will assist you when compiling your *Service Standards Checklist*.

Most of the points made in this book are common sense. However, as Mahatma Ghandi says, 'Common sense is not common!', yet sometimes it just takes a fresh pair of eyes and a new approach.

Being renowned for Exceptional Service makes business sense.

The exercises at the end of some of the chapters will ask you what you do well. Celebrate these with your team and encourage them to maintain these service levels and behaviours. Be aware of what you and your team do well and feel great about it.

Now let's consider who your customer is and what they want, need and like.

STAGE 1.
ALL CUSTOMERS

Getting the basics in place for 'all customers'.

WHO IS YOUR
CUSTOMER?

Before you even contemplate what exceptional is for your business, it is important to consider what you are striving to achieve for your customers.

What do your customers want from you? More to the point, who is your customer? We often forget about our customers yet, as already stated, they are THE most important people in keeping our businesses buoyant. The exercise at the end of the previous chapter will have given you a start by encouraging you to list the outcomes you want for your customers. The following questions will take these thoughts a little deeper. Who are these people leaving your business with those thoughts and feelings?

CONSIDER:

- Who wants and/or needs your product and/or service?
- Are you offering a product as a professional service (i.e. business to business) or a leisure service to enhance people's lifestyle?
- How do your customers live?
- What basic expectations do they have?

CONSIDER WHAT YOUR CUSTOMERS ARE LOOKING FOR:

- Service
- Knowledge
- Expertise
- Accuracy
- The 'WOW' factor
- Confidence
- Guidance
- Health
- Reassurance

- Information
- Cleanliness
- An experience
- Luxury
- Relaxation
- An informal approach
- Pace
- Efficiency
- Adherence to legislation

To assist you with your thinking, consider one of your customers and your perspective of them. Capture what you believe is most important to them.

Please don't restrict your thinking, and use additional paper if needed.

Once you have a better understanding of your customers, it is useful to reflect on where your business started and how this has influenced your business today. You may be going back decades or centuries, or you could only be thinking of the last 12 months if your business is relatively new. It is worth considering how this history has enabled your business growth.

Here are a couple of examples of business who are very clear about what was and is still important to them.

The Savoy, London, has a rich history, and the team is very proud of this heritage for many reasons, one of which is being the first to do so many things which other hotels have since emulated. There have been many well-known guests who have made history whilst staying at the hotel. These stories are told by the team to bring the magic of The Savoy from the 19th century alive today. This was the case when I worked there and is still the case today. The team at The Savoy embraces its history and is proud to be playing their part in its future.

Another example, Bents Garden and Home, is a family business that is currently in its third generation. Whilst their business has developed and grown over the years, their core focus remains as it was from day one, which is all about community. This is shared with the team from the beginning of their employment. I would say there is no doubt in the team's mind what the aspiration was and still is.

In order to build trust with your customers, it is important that everyone behaves in a way that is aligned to your company ambitions and culture, balanced with building a track record of delivering great results. In business you employ and value the diversity of your team. With this diversity comes people with individual beliefs of how things should be done. This is when conflict appears within businesses, where individuals think things are to be done their way. It is helpful for everyone to have clarity in how we do things 'around here'.

Many successful organisations shape their business by having values. These communicate to their teams the character of the business. When the employees behave in a way that is aligned to the company's values and culture, then the true essence of the business is brought to life. It is important that all leaders lead by example in demonstrating these values, otherwise confusion is created within your business. This confusion will then lead to a lack of trust within the workforce. When your employees/colleagues are clear, are fully engaged and aligned to the culture of your business, they (generally speaking) will influence the results positively. This competence is important when shaping your reputation. When people live your values and deliver the required results, trusting relationships with your customers (and everyone else within your business) will flourish and grow.

This culture would align to your customers and what's important to them too.

Here's an example of an organisation whose culture was so strong that everyone knew its values, lived them and the impact it had. It all came from the top.

The Chairman and CEO of this hotel chain would talk about the values at every opportunity when presenting to the staff. Awards were presented to those people who had excelled in living the values. The great things the award winner had done were shared when the awards were presented. This inspired others to follow suit. Customers loved the company brand, and visitors to the business would comment on the friendliness and care between the team members. The business results grew and grew, year on year. The team knew what they needed to do to deliver amazing results and did so—and more importantly, they wanted to. They loved working there.

The secret is to maintain focus on the culture and the results will take care of themselves. (almost!)

So, moving on to your business...

CONSIDER:

- What was the intention when your business was established?
- Is this intention still relevant today?
- What was important to your customers then?
- Are any of these still relevant to your customers today?
- What are the important characteristics of your business that will shape your culture?
- What is important that everyone in your business understands? i.e. this is how we do things around here.
- Do you have values that guide you and your team? If so, are they lived by everyone? If not, what will you do about this?
- Do you and all leaders within your business live the values to show and guide others?
- What would it be like if everyone in your business lived these values? What impact would this have on the outcomes or results within your business?

If you are part of a large organisation and not clear what the business ambitions and intentions are or were, base your answers on what you do know.

We know that happy customers return and will make recommendations to others. If every person in an organisation puts looking after their customers at the heart of everything they do, it's likely to have a positive impact. A good starting point is to consider what you would want if you were a customer in your business. However, don't stick to your expectations, as many of your customers are possibly not like you! Ask your customers what they are expecting as they use your product or service. I'm sure you can carry out this exercise based on the customers you interact with each and every day.

CONSIDER:

- What is your current reputation?
- What do people say about you now and over the past year?
- What is being said about your business on social media?
- What is being said on feedback sites?
- Are you proud of what people are saying?
- What would being proud of the things people are saying do for your reputation and the success of your business?

Once you have an idea of what your customers are looking for, you can start creating the product and experience they want and more. However, it will take some time to get there as you will have to ensure that you and your team fully understand what exceptional service and results look and feel like. Everyone needs to buy in to the process.

This is not a one-off process. It is also important to constantly challenge yourself to remain relevant to the wants and needs of your customers. The priorities of the company may also change, so you may need to evolve accordingly.

CONSIDER:

First of all, you need to be clear about what you want to achieve for your customers and business. To consolidate this chapter, consider the following questions. The answers will form the starting point for upgrading the service you offer.

- What outcome do you want for your customers?
- What is important to your customers?
- Are you clear about the market you are in? Who are you trying to attract to your business?
- What do you advertise or tell others about your business? Is this a true reflection of what actually happens?
- What are your customers saying about you?
- Ask your customers what they would like to see more of within your business.
- Are you proud of your business, its product and service?
- What do you want to do to make your business, product or service even better?

If you don't know the answers to these questions, ask. Talk to the long-serving colleagues within your team or maybe your boss or a family member if you work in a family-run business. However, if you give this due time and thought, you will realise you know more than you give yourself credit for. I think most people who are with their customers day in and day out will know the answers to most of these questions from how their customers behave and what they ask for.

Who is your customer?

Understanding who your customer is will assist you as you create the exceptional experience you want for them. It's important to remember it's about your customer, not you. Have these thoughts in your mind as you progress through the book.

WHAT OUR CUSTOMERS **WANT TO SEE**

More often than not, what your customers see creates their first impression. First impressions count and they last. People hold these memories as a mental photograph. It takes 18 further interactions to change someone's first impression of you or your business. This is, of course, if your customers return after their first visit or interaction to give you a second chance.

What we see has a big impact on our perceptions. When we travel through towns and villages and we see the streets being swept, bins emptied, pavements washed and weeds non-existent, it gives a sense of care and pride within the community. It is no different with a business.

Being in our businesses daily can mean we become complacent and comfortable with how things look. We can be blind to the pile of paperwork on the desk, the dirty windows or the torn posters, or become so used to the way the website looks we cannot see obvious flaws. There are some business owners or senior leaders who don't visit their front-line business to consider the customer experience. They therefore are oblivious to what their customers see when they come to the premises. It is important to walk in and around your business with a purpose, not simply moving from one place to another. Walk and observe, considering whether what you see is what you want your customers to see and experience.

CONSIDER

- When do your customers start making an assessment of your business through what they see?
- Are you proud of what you see?
- Do your customers see what you want them to see? Is everything in good working order, looking clean, fresh and inviting?
- Is your product presented in a way that makes it easy for your customers to buy?
- Do your team look well presented, show interest and seem to care for your customers?

First impressions

To start, consider where your customer's experience begins. Is it when they search for your website? Or is it when they see you on online platforms? Maybe their experience starts when they walk through the door to your shop, office, holiday let or workshop? What is it they see that creates their first impression? When do they start to make a judgment whether they want to engage with your business?

Consider how each stage of your customer experience links to the next. Is what they see on your website a true reflection of what your business looks like? Is what you say they will experience actually what happens? They don't even need to experience it to find out. They can always take a look on social media and see what other people's first impressions are before deciding to visit.

We see so many things that create thoughts and feelings—good and bad. Here are just some examples of how what is seen may impact on your customer's perception of you, your team and your business. This has a direct impact on how your customers buy.

CONSIDER

Do your customers see:
- clear contact details?
- fit-for-purpose business premises?
- tidy and conscientious staff?
- neat corridors?
- a place where they feel welcomed and comfortable?

 CASE STUDY

Here's a little story of a well-known clothing retail outlet whose website worked well for me as their customer. I needed to change my account details, so I went to their website. The 'Contact us' button was easy to find (which, in my experience, is unique—they are often hidden!), it gave a choice of calling a number or asking if I'd like them to call me back at a specific time that suited me. This is great! I'm not used to having choice. What is even better is, if they don't answer when you call, you have the option of leaving a message. From first-hand experience, they do call back. If you choose for them to call you at a specific time to suit you, they do. What is also pleasing is that it is a person, a real, live human, who calls you back. They were friendly, helpful and addressed my queries effectively and efficiently.

Here's your first exercise to reflect on this story shared. Make the most of these throughout the book to give your own customer, team and business thorough consideration.

On reflection from this, consider:
- What impression do you have of this organisation?
- What do you believe they want their customers to experience?

Before thinking about your business, here are few of my thoughts:
- It was an easy and hassle-free experience.
- They want their customers to call them and want to assist them in any way that they can.
- They want to make it easy for the customers to make contact with them.
- They place the customer at the centre of their business and are flexible to call them at a time that suits the customer. They resolved my query effectively and efficiently, by listening and responding appropriately.
- I get the impression that this organisation has given their systems and processes careful consideration to ensure their customers receive a customer-centric, personalised and responsive experience.

Thinking about your business:
- How do your customers make contact with you and your business?
- Is it easy for your customers to find your contact details?
- Does what your customer see that is promised on your website, social media or your materials, mirror the reality of what they experience?
- What do your customers see as they approach your business?
- What systems and processes do you need to consider to ensure that your customers have received your ideal experience?

So many organisations make it difficult to speak to someone directly or to speak to anyone at all. What is slightly worrying is that this example was an unusual experience because it was so good. I could easily see how to contact them and they delivered on their promise to call back. Unfortunately, we are used to this not being the case. This is more than just what we see, it also about how people respond and follow up on what they say they will do.

I can't understand why any organisation would not want their customers to contact them.

When your customers have visited your website and potentially enjoyed a conversation with you or one or two of your team, their next encounter may be a visit to your premises in person. It's time to think about how your customers approach your business and where this starts; is it in the car park or on the street? In the property market, they call this curb appeal.

Recently, I saw an estate agent board outside a terraced house property that stated 'Luxury Apartments To Let', then lifted my eyes to see weeds growing around the edge of the walls of the property, and dirty, dusty windows and window frames. It made me question the word 'luxury' and made me doubt the honesty of that estate agent's marketing. Had the curb appeal been different, maybe I'd have been enticed to take a look.

With this example, I'm left thinking, 'Do the landlords want people to want to stay in their premises? Do they care for their tenants and potential tenants? Or do they want to take their money and run?' I've heard so many nightmare stories of landlords who don't maintain their properties, thereby risking their tenants' well-being, where damp, mould or leaks are apparent with nothing or very little being done about it. Would you want your property company to be considered negligent on first impression?

What do your customers see when they step into your business?

Those first impressions continue when someone enters your business. It is just as important that what the customer sees reflects positively on you and your company.

A solicitor I approached for business had an open office with the team working away at their desks, which were stacked with files bound with red tape. It looked cluttered and disorganised. The impression I had was that my file would potentially join those many files. Could I trust that they would find it? From what I saw, I suspected that it would be a long process, and my file was likely to go to the bottom. I didn't engage with them.

People notice the way we work. If your customers see chaos, mess or clutter, it sends negative signals. When areas are tidy and well-organised, where the staff seem calm and in control, it sends a positive message. This is the beginning of a potential ongoing relationship, as your customers build trust with you, your organisation and your team. Of course, it is not just about what they see as all the senses are interconnected; we will return to this point later.

CONSIDER

Think about the all the areas your customers see in your business:

- What do your customers see when they step into your business?
- Would you be proud to show it off to someone you truly want to impress?
- Does it have great curb appeal?
- Is it clean, fresh, tidy and clutter-free?
- Is it immaculate and in pristine condition?
- Is it in good repair?
- Is it fit for purpose?
- Do your customers get a sense of 'I'm the first to be here' or are there signs of the previous customer's debris?

Consider the people in your organisation. This is as important or even more important than getting your environment looking exceptional. If the people I see within an organisation don't seem to be able to look after themselves, or don't seem to be bothered, how can they possibly look after me?

People create the first impressions your customers see and experience.

The standards set need to be reviewed constantly. I remember investing in a new suit at a time when I had little disposable income. I then embarked on a mission to lose weight. This suit soon became too big and a colleague noticed this and suggested that I bought a suit that fitted me. On a closer look at myself, he was right. I looked sloppy and scruffy. A new suit (the right size) was purchased. It doesn't matter if you have big, little, tall or short people within your team, poorly fitting clothes look awful.

A few weeks ago, I arrived to work at a formal five-star hotel, which has a high profile and is steeped in history with an outstanding reputation. I approached the concierge, where a colleague was standing behind the desk. He was engaged in a conversation with a luggage porter who was leaning on the customer/guest side of the desk. I'd never seen this behaviour before in this hotel. I'm pretty sure the senior leaders in the team would not have liked this informal, laid-back approach. I walked up to the desk and asked if everything was alright. The porter said, 'Yeah, we're just catching up, having a good chat.' In my head I was saying 'Don't let me get in the way!' They didn't know the reason for my visit. What if I had been a paying customer, worth a potential fortune?

There are times when I walk into a business and the person behind the counter is on the phone, talking to another colleague, or leaning on the desk. It gives the impression that the customer is secondary. The message given is that the person on the end of the phone or the chat they are having with their colleague is their priority. The staff member is indicating that they will finish that before they even consider the waiting customer—the customer who is waiting to spend money with the organisation which is paying their wage. Is this happening in your business?

There are times when a customer is on the phone as another customer is looking for assistance in person. Experts who look after customers are able to use appropriate body language—such as eye contact, a nod, a smile—to acknowledge and re-assure the customer in front of them. This sends a friendly message that they will have their attention as soon as they have looked after the customer on the call.

The worst example I have seen of this behaviour is when I visit the gym—although this is not exclusive to the gym (or indeed all gyms), I see this in all businesses. As you walk in, the person behind the desk is staring at the computer. They don't look up to acknowledge you are there, and you may as well be invisible. I have stood there for a few seconds—although it feels like minutes—until they look up and act all surprised that a customer has entered their business. It amazes me! Are they not expecting customers to come in? Surely the purpose of these people is to look after the customer as their priority. The email or computer task can be done later. The person in front of you is your golden opportunity to impress.

On the next page is another real-life scenario with some questions for you to answer. I could quite easily go on forever as people play such a crucial role in making the customer experience exceptional or not.

Notes

CASE STUDY

Whilst purchasing a cake and coffee in a canteen-style eatery, it was all very pleasant until we moved along the line to pay. The person taking payment had a face like a wet weekend! Whilst I realise this person may have had things on her mind, as a customer who is enjoying a treat during their leisure time, this is not what I'd expect. I felt like saying 'Sort your face out'. I could sense that she was not happy and was probably having a negative impact on others in the team.

On reflection from this, consider:
- What impression do you have of this organisation?
- What do you believe the organisation wants their customers to experience?
- What impact do you believe the 'wet weekend face' person is having on her colleagues?
- How would you be feeling if you had been working alongside this unhappy person?

Before we consider your business, here are my thoughts:
- The colleague seemed to have no care for the customer.
- I was concerned that they had personal circumstances that were distracting them from their role. If this was the case, the front-line colleague would (or should) inform their leader or manager, who then could support them appropriately.
- The purpose of the front-line colleague is to look after the customer. It's like being 'on stage'. When we visit the theatre, the actors play the part aligned to the script, so that the audience leaves having enjoyed the show. There is no difference. The audience or customers simply want to have a great experience. What is going on 'backstage' or any personal problems should not be an issue for the customers. They don't want to know. Nor should they.
- Customers don't expect this kind of attitude to be thrown at them. All they want is to have a pleasant experience, buy from you and spend money.
- Customers should be dealt with in a friendly and polite manner as a minimum. We are all very good at reading the body language of others.
- It's important to think about what the customer wants to see and experience at all times and consistently.
- I believe the colleagues were drained by the unhappy person. I got the impression that they were feeling as though they were walking on eggshells whilst being around her.
- Not knowing what was potentially wrong or upsetting the mood of the unhappy colleague, if I had been working with her, I would have asked if she was alright. I think some people are not aware that they a creating an atmosphere by their perceived mood.

- Then I would see what could be done to assist my upset colleague, and maybe make short-term adjustments to meet the needs of the situation. This would be with the aim of helping them, the team, the customers and the business. If the colleague can't behave appropriately around customers, perhaps this isn't the right job role for them. Offering good customer service is a skill, not everybody can do it.

- If you don't like working with customers, don't. The customers can tell and it will impact on business eventually. It doesn't make sense, business sense.

Thinking about your business:

- How would you like your team to be seen by your customers?

- What behaviours would you like your team to show? Do you and your team demonstrate these behaviours?

- If so, have you shown them appreciation for what they are doing well?

- If not, what have you done to understand what might be stopping you and your team from showing these behaviours?

- What might be happening behind the scenes that you're not aware of or haven't considered?

- What do you think your team might want or need from you to guide and support them in delivering the service you expect for all your customers?

- Are your team committed to delivering exceptional service to your customers?

- What are you going to do to establish whether they are committed or not?

- What will you do to ensure your whole team is showing your customers positive attitudes and behaviours that inspire them to return?

Remember: customers first, tasks and
internal conversations second.

The first point here is that your team needs to be seen in order to create a good first impression. If they are not present, this opportunity is lost and never to be experienced again. How a person presents themselves via their body language accounts for 55%[1] of the message that is being sent to others—your customers in this case. This includes looking clean, smart, well presented and well groomed. Positive body language is crucial: facial expressions, eye contact, posture, standing up straight (i.e. not leaning) and positive hand gestures. People who are emotionally in tune will notice these things.

A former colleague of mine used to say about the five-star hotel world that colleagues need to remember which entrance they use to get into the hotel. In other words, all colleagues are to enter the hotel via the 'staff entrance'. However, even though this is the case, some colleagues seem to have thoughts above their station as though they are paying customers. Such people can at times frown upon the non-VIP, non-celebrity or low tipping clients. Who do they think they are? This is the case with other industries too, where the staff have no expression, almost looking down their noses at the customer, as can be the case in some solicitors, accountants, retail boutiques and private banking. I think people who act like this need to have a big reality check.

All customers, no matter who they are, are critical to your business. Making judgement of them is a waste of energy and will have a negative impact on your business.
They are important. Remember that!

CONSIDER:

- Are your team aligned to how you want your business to be presented to your customers?
- Do your team look proud to work for your business and are they an ambassador for your business?
- What do people see you and your team doing?
- How do your colleagues stand, or do they lean?
- Do you and your team look clean and well presented, and aligned to the image of your business?
- Does the clothing they wear fit them?
- Do they look genuinely happy to help customers, or anybody for that matter?

---

1   According to Dr Albert Mehrabian's 'Elements of Personal Communication theory'

What do your customers see that makes it easy for them to purchase your products or services?

How do most customers purchase from you? It may be when your customer is in your business in person or might be via your website. In both instances, displaying what is available and making it easy to purchase is a must. Can you make it easier for customers to buy from you?

An example of this is when you see the mobile drink servers at busy sporting events or concerts, where they carry the drink in a backpack tank. The drinks come to you rather than the spectators having to join a huge queue at the bar. It's fabulous! I'm sure their takings are high as it's so easy to spend money as a customer.

Walking into a café that presents their options on blackboards or clear menus so you are tempted by their tasty offerings makes it easy for the customer. They take your initial order as soon as you arrive. That's if you're ready, of course. It's funny how a coffee turns into coffee plus an irresistible cake or pastry if the process of ordering is easy and the temptation is set out in front of you! That one coffee and cake soon turns into two when there is attentive and efficient service.

When staff are friendly, engaging and seem to want to help you, when they give good eye contact, are calm and share information, it often leads customers to buy.

Frequently, we see staff around, yet they don't offer to help. When we, as customers, have to raise our head or hand or look for a member of staff to get their attention, I believe the service provider has failed. This often happens in a restaurant when we want to pay the bill. It seems the staff have gone off duty as you've finished your meal. It's as though you're no longer there! You see them, but they don't seem to see you. This is also the case in food halls and supermarkets, where employees would prefer to work on their tasks rather than look after the customer. They seem so engrossed (or purposefully blinkered) in stacking or arranging the stock, that they are not at all interested in selling it! Customers want to see an instant response as they gaze for assistance. After all, they are trying to buy your product and services! Don't you want to be paid or make a sale? It's a fine balance. The key is to notice your customer and give appropriate attention when the customer wants and needs it.

We enjoy being focused on a task as once it's complete, **we** gain a sense of satisfaction. However, looking after our customers first, gives **them** a sense of satisfaction. Assisting **them** has a greater positive longer-term impact than our mini victory of a task being complete. Remember, this is all about **them** not **us**.

CONSIDER:

- What do your customers see that makes it easy for them to purchase your products or services?
- Do you and your team ask how you can help as soon as possible so your customers can respond appropriately? Or do you and your team welcome customers into your business so your customers know who to go to in case they want or need help?
- Are you and your team attentive towards your customers?
- Do you and your team keep a caring eye on your customers?
- Do you and your team look calm and happy to help?
- Do you and your team make it easy for your customer to spend money?

A bit more about cleanliness– especially toilets

Here's a big gripe of many people across the world: toilets, especially in eateries. Dirty, poorly maintained loos are terrible. The toilet is the place where our customers are left alone to examine part of your customer experience. What experience do you want them to have? What is often seen is dirty loos? No toilet paper, a grimy toilet seat which is falling off, no effective hand drying facilities, the flooring wet and/or stained. We're not in the dark ages, this is the 21st century; basic toilet visits shouldn't feel like going to an old bog!

What is going through your customers' minds if the area where you allow them to visit isn't cared for? Probably 'What is happening in the areas they don't allow us to visit, such as the kitchen?' They wonder if you can't keep the toilets looking good, how is it where the food is prepared? If the toilets are looking awful, how many customers never visit again or maybe leave before ordering? We shall be re-visiting the toilet experience a couple of times through the book, as you can imagine it is not only what you see that is an issue in this part of your premises!

Clean areas and surfaces are not just about the toilets. You need to consider all areas of your business. Seeing thick dust on food products in food stores is very off-putting. How long have they been there? It's the same in toy and stationery stores too.

Having recently visited a shopping centre early in the morning, it made my heart sing—and not just because it was a retail opportunity! The centre was being cleaned and the person cleaning was thoroughly wiping down a child's ride, ensuring all the touch points were thoroughly attended to, to reduce the spread of infection. It looked fabulous by the time she had finished. It was gleaming and all sparkly. I'm sure many children and parents would have been drawn to the ride.

What we see builds trust. Seeing a five rating for hygiene on the door of a place to eat builds my confidence that it's safe to eat there and I'm less likely to leave feeling sick. Look at the Fire Service: in my experience, I've never seen a dirty, untidy fire station, engine or officer (and I've looked hard, believe me!). They all appear smart, organised and well presented. This is all part of their intense training, which leads to them performing when we need them.

CONSIDER:

- Do you and your team look clean, smart and well presented?
- Are they in the correct style of clothing or uniform aligned to your business style and aspirations?
- Are all surfaces within your business cleaned and well-maintained?
- Would you rate yourself and your premises 10 out of 10 for cleanliness, curb appeal, well-presented and smart staff?
- Are you proud of what you see?

Are you and your team trained to deliver exceptional standards each and every day?

Seeing it all come together

To summarise, it's important to walk through your customer's journey from beginning to end. It needs to be easy to make contact with your business. What your customers see on your website needs to be a true reflection of reality. As your customers arrive at your premises, do you feel proud of what you see and confident that all aspects will look well-maintained and immaculate? Getting the team to look happy, calm, clean, tidy, well presented and delighted to look after anyone within your business is the ultimate of ultimate—and of course, ensuring everyone makes it easy for customers to spend money with you.

One last good example that brings the environment, team and sale together.

I was purchasing a fitting for the shower. Our neighbour was helping us and he researched the item on a national DIY store. He selected the item, ordered it online from the local store, which indicated the item was in stock and when it would be ready for collection. I collected it on the day stated. The car park was clean and tidy, the doors were clean, free from smears and dirt. There were two well-presented people behind the counter, in uniform. One person was already with a customer, the second acknowledged me straight away with a big smile and asked how she could help. All the shelves behind the counter looked clean, tidy and well organised. The information was shared and the item collected. All the staff were pleasant. I asked about returning the product if it was not the right item. The staff member explained the fair terms and conditions, then asked if she could help with anything else, was polite, helpful and friendly. I paid. The overall experience was professional, efficient, effective and a pleasure. This is the place to go!

Notes

See Exceptional

The examples in the following checklist are to guide you to think exceptional. Your business may already be at this level, which is fabulous. If it is, I have a challenge for you: how can you maintain this?

If your business is not at this exceptional level and you have not looked at your business in this detail before, simply assess where your business is at the moment. Take one or two points to make the changes doable and easy to maintain. The challenge is then to gradually upgrade your service over time, so that you are confident that you and your team are performing at a consistently high level.

SEE EXCEPTIONAL CHECKLIST

Take a walk around your business. Look at your website. Consider these questions and make a list of the things that you do well.

See exceptional service standards

Website and Social Media:

Are you proud of your website?	Y ☐	N ☐
Is your website a true representative of your business?	Y ☐	N ☐
Is it easy for your customers to make contact with you?	Y ☐	N ☐
Would you want to buy from your business?	Y ☐	N ☐

Outside your business:

When your customers arrive at your business, do they see gleaming, clean windows with no dust, streaks, smears, handprints or water marks on them?	Y ☐	N ☐
When your customers arrive at your business, do they see attractive displays, a clean environment, healthy plants, etc.? Is it free from weeds and debris?	Y ☐	N ☐
Is the door opened for customers?	Y ☐	N ☐
Is the door clean? Free from fingerprints?	Y ☐	N ☐
Are all areas in working order? Are all lamps working?	Y ☐	N ☐
Do they see high hygiene scores where applicable?	Y ☐	N ☐

Inside and throughout your business:

Do your customers see a colleague who is focused on them and offering an instant, warm and genuine welcome? Y ☐ N ☐

Do your customers see positive staff interactions between each other? Y ☐ N ☐

Do your customers see colleagues giving instant warm eye contact, standing straight and showing caring body language towards them? Y ☐ N ☐

Are your team well presented, looking smart and aligned to the company image? Y ☐ N ☐

Do you and your customers see all colleagues moving around the business at an appropriate pace that looks calm and confident? i.e. not rushed or over relaxed Y ☐ N ☐

Do your customers see immaculate seating? Tabletops, bases and seats free from dust, crumbs and debris? Y ☐ N ☐

Do your customers see soft furnishings plumped up as though no-one else has been there? Y ☐ N ☐

Do your customers see freshly vacuumed, swept or mopped flooring? Free from debris, dust, dirt or grease? Y ☐ N ☐

Do your customers see clean vents and air filters that are free from dust and dirt? In a fully effective working order? Y ☐ N ☐

Do your customers see all literature immaculately presented, that is neat and tidy? Free from graffiti, rips and creases? Y ☐ N ☐

Do your customers see a well-maintained area? Free from scuffs on the paintwork? Are all lamps and lights in working order? Y ☐ N ☐

Do your customers see the information they want and need on immaculate materials? Free from creases, debris, graffiti, rips? Y ☐ N ☐

Do your customers see positive interactions with other customers? Are all colleagues being helpful to all customers? Y ☐ N ☐

Do your customers see all colleagues giving their undivided attention to the customer they are interacting with? Listening careful and responding appropriately? Y ☐ N ☐

Do your customers see all colleagues prioritising the customer before tasks and their colleagues? Y ☐ N ☐

Do your customers see all decorations in your business are clean, sparkling, fresh and well maintained? Do they see decorations that are aligned to the season? Y ☐ N ☐

Do your customers see all crockery and glassware immaculate? Free from cracks, chips, stains and water marks?   Y ☐   N ☐

Do your customers see immaculate cutlery? Free from debris, water stains and smears?   Y ☐   N ☐

Do your customers see healthy plants and flowers?   Y ☐   N ☐

Do your customers see helpful notices which are well placed? Or do colleagues guide the customer in person to the correct place?   Y ☐   N ☐

Do your customers see clean and inviting toilet facilities? Sparkling clean and free from stains and excessive water around the sinks?   Y ☐   N ☐

Do you customers see in cupboards, behind curtains, under beds or furniture, in walkways that are clean, free from clutter and debris?   Y ☐   N ☐

Notice the wording of these questions are stating the required standard, which would ideally be answered with a 'Yes'. This is important to gauge your scores moving forward.

Which of the these do you already do consistently?

    Celebrate what you notice you and your team do well. Encourage them to maintain this consistently. If you are leading a team, let them know what they do well, with the intention of creating a feel-good factor and great performance. This is likely to lead them to continue to deliver these great standards, as they know that they are being noticed for good reasons. This will also help you to engage your team with your mission of wanting to upgrade their performance to be exceptional. If you are considering your own performance and are delivering standards at this level, congratulate yourself and feel proud of what you do. Most of all, keep doing it—your customers will notice sooner or later.

Select the two service standards you want to upgrade or improve within your business and note them here:

1.

2.

———————

You will find a blank service standards checklist form in Appendix B.

Add the two points you have chosen to improve in your blank service standards checklist; you can build on this as you read through the next chapters. Perhaps you would like to share this with your team. Explain to them that you are wanting to maintain or upgrade your reputation with your customers. This will then lead to everyone becoming confident in your organisation's consistent high standard, so everyone feels reassured that they are on track. This will give you something to be looking out for as you start to build your own confidence and the confidence of your team. Do not use it to discipline anyone, only to guide them into understanding what good looks like.

In the later part of the book, when we take these basic sensory standards to become emotionally exceptional, you can upgrade the observation sheet accordingly.

Here is an example of how it would look.

SERVICE STANDARDS CHECKLIST		YES/ NO
1	**Does the entrance have an attractive curb appeal?** *(See)*	No
	What did you observe/notice? Weeds around the edge of the building and in the gutter in front of our premises. The windows were smeared and there were weeds next to the business signage.	
2	**Are all colleagues looking clean, smart and well presented?** *(See)*	Yes
	What did you observe/notice? Jane and Richard in clean company uniform. Ironed shirts and no stains.	

'See' is an all-consuming sense that has a big impact on consumers. There are several sayings that imply this, such as 'We eat with our eyes', or 'Our eyes are bigger than our belly'. Our sight also has the same effect when we see something we don't want to eat. With expressions like 'I don't like to look of that,' yet these foods often taste amazing. That was all rather food-orientated! However, I think it makes the point.

First impressions are so important throughout your customer's whole journey. It's worth taking a walk in their shoes. Take a good look at your website, online presence and premises. Cleanliness, tidiness and impressiveness is what you're looking for. There's nothing like seeing well-presented and attentive people when you need a product or service. It's even better for you, the provider (vendor), when these attentive people make it easy for your customer to spend their money and ensure there's cash in the bank. This will then keep your business buoyant.

Share with your team or colleague what you are striving to achieve, encourage them to get involved and make appropriate adjustments as you go along. You will soon see some positive differences being made.

This is just the beginning of our journey. We shall now examine 'hear'.

WHAT OUR CUSTOMERS WANT TO HEAR

Moving on to our second sense—hear—which has so many aspects to consider. This sense is particularly important to get right relating to the type of customers you have or that you want to attract. The acoustics play an important part. Taste in background sounds and expectations about what customers expect to hear will vary for differing age groups, cultures and circumstances. This variation might be more important for hear than the other senses.

Take a moment now and tune in to what you can hear. Is it a positive sound or not? Is it what you would expect for where you are?

When talking about hear, it is also about 'read', which sends a message linked to what your customer sees and leads to them 'hearing' your message.

What I find interesting with sound is that I pay little attention to it, yet when it doesn't work it changes my whole experience. Many people are unaware of the impact of sound on a conscious level but it has an impact subconsciously. For some people with good hearing, this impact can be huge. I have friends who will go to particular bars because of the music that is played. Not everyone's tastes are the same, which is why it's important to understand which customer you are striving to attract, as explained in Chapter 1.

CONSIDER:

- What do your customers hear as they have contact with your business?
- What do you want them to hear?
- How does what they hear complement the overall experience you want them to have?
- Do your customers hear things which are having a negative impact on their overall experience?
- What do your customers read that is or is not aligned to what you are striving to achieve?

First impressions

As with what is seen,

What can be heard as you enter premises can make or break a first impression.

Everything else in the experience could be perfect, but what is heard could put the customer off. Sometimes it is best not to have any background music at all.

Notes

CASE STUDY

There are two garden centres local to where I live; they are at totally different ends of the spectrum when it comes to customer experience. Yet the basic products they sell are identical. At the exceptional garden centre the whole experience is wonderful, its displays are amazing, the plants look healthy and cared for, it always has something new, on trend, and the food is delicious. A number of years ago, the only thing that would irritate me was the music they would play. It was like being by the seaside in the 1920's: it was outdated and, for me, depressing and not energising at all. I'm pleased to say this is no longer the case.

On reflection from this, consider:
- What would your first impressions have been of the background music?
- Would you have noticed it or not?

Before thinking about your business, here are a few of my thoughts:
- If you're wanting to be exceptional, all aspects of your customers' experience need to be considered.
- I'm glad they gave the background music their attention.
- The music was initially contradictory to the overall experience, whilst the other garden centre doesn't give it any attention at all.

Thinking about your business:
- What background music or noise do your customers experience?
- Is this aligned to your overall ambition for your customers?
- What could be the one or two things you might do to make an improvement?

The volume of any background music also needs to be considered. Some people like to hear music to add to the experience. For example, young people enjoy the music in clothes shops as it gets them in the mood when buying clothes for their Saturday night out. Whilst others want to ensure they can hold a conversation and hear what each other are saying.

Background music is becoming more prolific, and in some places there has been a bit of a backlash, with some deciding not to bother as a result. The time of day is also important to take into account.

I once stayed in a hotel where the heavy classical background music being played whilst having breakfast, although it was aligned to the style of hotel, was solemn and not at all appropriate for the time of day. Although music plays an important part in setting the scene, you don't want it to be overwhelming for those who are not morning people. It is tricky to get it right.

What about the music and instructions heard in a lift? We have an option to make this informative and positive for our customers. We have our customers' attention during this time. What message would you like them to receive whilst in the lift to take this from a mundane experience to an exceptional, uplifting, informative one?

In a hotel where I used to work, mini screens were placed in the lift, playing comedy sketches or cartoons. It put a smile on our guests' faces and created connections with the people using the lift—it was a talking point. This is an exceptional example of what people see and hear.

CONSIDER:

- Do you have background music or noises that complement the experience you want for your customers?
- Do you have distracting noises that might irritate or frustrate your customers? These might be noises that you have become used to, so strive to have a fresh pair of ears when reflecting on this.
- Are you clear about the experience you want your customers to have?

On the phone

Of course, there's that lovely 'on hold' music we have the privilege of listening to as a customer! Alongside this is the message that is often repeated whilst waiting. It is so annoying and drives me bonkers, as I'm sure it does you too. I'm not sure why organisations think it's acceptable to do this; after all, the people calling you are the most precious element of your business—your customer. Here's a quick reminder of why your customer is important to you— they pay your wages and keep your business afloat so that you can maintain the lifestyle that you choose. (I did say this would be mentioned a number of times!) What I hear on the phone with many organisations does not give me the impression that they care at all.

The 'on hold' music varies between businesses. I've experienced music that seems best suited to a funeral director, whilst I have to confess that I quite enjoy the choice of music of some companies, especially if it is varied and not the same track playing over and over again. Let's face it, there are times when we are left on hold for long periods of time—10, 20, 30 minutes—and that's a long time to be listening to bad electronic music on a loop!

Whilst I'm on the subject of phone calls, the message we hear whilst on hold is often contradictory to what we are experiencing. I often hear 'Thank you for you call. Your call is important to us, please hold the line, a customer agent will be with you shortly.' In reality, I've heard this over 20 times whilst I've been waiting. Is this what your customers are hearing when they call your business?

When was the last time you called your own organisation to understand what your customers have to do to use your business?

Many organisations seem to think that it's all right for customers to talk to robots, that an automated experience is what their customers want. Your call is answered by a pre-recorded voice, then you're given a choice of departments you might want to talk to and you have to select the appropriate department you want or think you want. This is not putting the customer at the centre of your business.

The additional frustrations with these phone experiences are two-fold:

1. When we eventually get to speak to the service agent we require and we can't understand what they are saying, which can be garbled and clearly following a script (we shall consider this later in the chapter).

2. We're sometimes asked to enter our account number and other personal details on our keypad. (This leaves me feeling unsure of where my data is going and I don't trust them.) Then when the service agent is on the line eventually (Sometimes we don't get to speak to a human at all and I personally think this is awful!), they ask us for all the personal information again. What a total waste of time! And where does that information go?

The perfect phone experience would be to call an organisation with the phone answered within three rings, with a genuine greeting that is understood by the caller.

The customer should be able to ask for what they need and to be connected directly to the right person. Should a message need to be taken, the contact details would be noted, along with a brief outline of what the customer needs. These details would be confirmed with the caller to reassure them that the correct details have been taken. The caller would be asked for the best time for the correct person to call back. The magic takes place when the right person calls the customer back at the specified time, introduces themselves and links the purpose of the call to what they have asked for. This is far more efficient and effective and places your customer at the heart of all that you do.

The customers should not need to repeat their request or requirements.

As there have been many moans up to now, I'd like to say a bit about the organisations who get it right.

CASE STUDY

I had an appointment with a personal shopper in a fabulous department store. I didn't know where to go when I arrived at the door. I was standing outside the store and rang them. A person answered straight away and I explained what I needed. They responded with 'Oh great, I've just seen Jenny. She was on the second floor, away from her department. May I place you on hold to make sure she is still there, rather than putting you through to the wrong place?' I agreed. He came back to me to say that he had found her and was about to connect me. He also said, 'Happy shopping.' We were connected. It was efficient and effective and left me thinking how friendly and caring he was. I felt valued, considered, cared for and was looking forward to my shopping experience. Which meant, by the way, that I spent more money than I had anticipated! I've returned to the store many times since for a personal shopping experience and intend to continue to do so, whilst also recommending this to family and friends.

Using the example from above:
- How would you have felt as the customer?

My thoughts from this experience are as follows:
- I remember this even though it was several years ago.
- I'm loyal to this store and it's my first choice when I purchase clothing.
- Small things like this make a huge difference.
- I felt as though I had the person's undivided attention. I was listened to, valued and cared for. I know of at least three friends who have since used the service after me telling them about my experience.

Consider your business:
- What experience do your customers have when they call your organisation?
- Does the person answering calls give one-to-one focused attention to each and every caller?
- Do you believe your customer would feel valued having called and spoken to people in your team?
- When was the last time you listened carefully to a call between a colleague and a customer?

As already highlighted, it seems that some organisations don't want to talk to their customers. I understand that times can be tough and staffing is an expensive luxury, BUT the importance of the customer needs to be considered to keep those tough times at bay.

However, it's another story when companies want to talk to you: we receive messages via all kinds of sources (e.g. emails, texts) asking for feedback. Again, these messages tell us our feedback is important to them, yet how they treat us as customers seem contradictory.

CONSIDER:

- Do you and you team have an agreed greeting when you answer the phone, one that showcases your business as you'd like?
- Do you have a standard that outlines the timings when a call is to be answered? i.e. within 3 rings.
- Are you and your team clear about the experience you want your customer to have when on the phone?
- What background noise are your customers hearing whilst on the phone to any person within your business?
- Do you and your colleagues give all customers on the phone your undivided attention? Focusing only on the caller.
- How often do your customers phone your business?
- What is your message-taking procedure?
- Are all messages that are taken from your customers responded to as you'd like?

What is heard from within your business?

Returning to the experience your customers have whilst in your business—what additional sounds are they exposed to?

In your business, what do your customers hear that perhaps they don't want to hear? This includes things like doors banging, hand dryers, toilets flushing, machinery whizzing, staff clattering cutlery or crockery, traffic, drilling, banging, screaming children, animal noises (There's a hotel I know that is located next to a zoo!), and so the list goes on.

This is also applicable to what your customers hear when they are on the phone to your business. Our customers only want to hear what they want to hear. To put this into context, should I want to hold a business meeting I would want to have the attention of the participants, for them not to be distracted unnecessarily during the meeting. When planning the meeting, I wouldn't ask for the room to be quiet. Yet if you experience distracting noise during a meeting (even in the most beautiful environment), it is not acceptable.

Likewise, when in a professional service, you don't want to overhear what is being said or experienced with other clients. We don't want to hear the treatment of others—for example in the dentist, doctors, solicitors or accountants—as we want privacy.

In exceptional organisations, what is heard and experienced by customers is carefully considered. They ensure their service is discreet, elegant, and that operational activity is not a distraction. An example of this is when you dine in a restaurant or drink in a bar in an exceptional establishment: the drinks, cutlery and crockery are placed in front of you with no sound—not plonked or slammed down. It creates a totally different experience for the customer. This, I believe, can be implemented by any style of drinking or eating outlet where elegance is adopted. It is pure bliss.

What our team say and how they say it

Exceptional service is all about the people delivering the service. What they say and how they say it is crucial in creating the experience you want your customers to have.

What is said is important. The words are critical, despite the statistics stating that words are only 7% of message received, with 38% being **how** it is said, i.e. tone of voice.

Often we hear people in organisations saying what they are expected to say, yet **how** it is said is almost robotic, garbled and said in a way that is sometimes not understood or sincere. This can be on the phone or face to face. It is important to remember what is being said and the reason for it.

I have been guilty of getting this wrong. I used to answer my phone in the department where I worked in a rushed manner. The standard our company adopted to answering the phone was to include the following aspects: 'Good morning/afternoon/evening, thank you for calling (the department), (our name) speaking, how may I help you?' I knew that I'd rushed my greeting by the caller's response, which was 'Thank you, Ali, for your help.' I used to think 'Ali? Who is Ali?' I soon realised they hadn't heard me state 'Sally' as all my words ran into the next. Shame on me!

Consider how things are said

Now on to the manner in which things are said in your business. Consider things like the inflection used (how you emphasise certain words), the pace of your speech, the pitch of your voice and the volume. Is it appropriate for your business?

Inflection: The words that are being emphasised and the modulation in your voice has a big impact on how a message is received.

CONSIDER

Is what you are saying said in the way that you mean it? Are the important words emphasised? Here's a little exercise for you to see what this means. Read the following sentence out loud to yourself, then place greater emphasis on the highlighted word in each of the variations. What would you understand from how it is said?

I didn't say she stole the money.

1: **I** didn't say she stole the money
What would be understood? It wasn't me who said this, it might have been someone else.

2: I **didn't** say she stole the money
What would be understood? I didn't say this.

3: I didn't **say** she stole the money
What would be understood? I didn't say this, although I might have thought it or implied this.

4: I didn't say **she** stole the money
What would be understood? I said someone stole the money, not necessarily 'her'.

5: I didn't say she **stole** the money
What would be understood? I said she might have taken or borrowed the money.

6: I didn't say she stole the **money**
What would be understood? I said she might have stolen something else.

What you will find is that how something is said gives it a different meaning. You might have experienced this when you have said something yet the person you were speaking to does something not aligned to what you have said.

When asking them, they respond with 'You said this.' Often, you did say what they've repeated, but you didn't mean it in that way. This can be the cause of unnecessary conflict.

We need to ensure we say things in the way that we mean.

This requires us to think about what we are about to say before we say it. 'Put your brain in gear before opening your mouth' is good advice!

Pace: Ensure that you speak at a pace that can be understood. This is where less is more. Be clear and to the point about what you want to say. (I've relearned this whilst writing this book!) Apply the commas and full stops within your sentences as you speak. What this does is allow the person listening to digest what is being said. The pace needs to be just right. Not too fast, as all the words blend into one. Not too slow, where the listener is falling asleep or feeling agitated as you're not getting to the point.

Pitch: Choose your pitch so it is aligned to what you are saying, high or low. Generally speaking, a high pitch is related to positivity and joy. For example, when you see someone you're delighted to see, you would greet them with a higher pitch of 'Hi, how are you?' with lots or spring, zest and energy. However, when you want to be grounded, calm or concerned you would lower your tone, saying something like 'Good morning, how are you?' Be aware of your body language and facial expression. Vary your tone and what is said to reflect what is presented to you. If you want to be credible, you would align yourself with the needs of the person with whom you are communicating, whilst remaining genuine, warm and realistic, not contrived or fake.

An example of this was in an American diner in the United States. We were greeted with a high pitch 'Hi, good to see you.' This is great. However, it continued as the person serving us introduced themselves in a high pitch: 'Hi, my name is Dee. I will be your server today.' It came across as being false and totally forced. This was a turning point for me with my perception of service in the United States not being genuine. A lower pitch shows your sincerity. A more serious situation requires a deeper pitch. This needs to be right.

Volume: Getting the volume right when communicating with others is also important. When speaking too loud, it is possible to lose the emphasis and tone of the message; too quiet and you can't hear what is being said. Overall, what is said needs to be at a volume that can easily be understood by the recipient. This is basic, yet so many people get it wrong. A handy hint: people who have difficultly hearing generally need the pace and inflection of how you are speaking to be altered, not the volume. Likewise, for people who are not English speaking. Slow down, be clear, concise and maintain eye contact with them. Eye contact is important on the phone too. Whilst you can't look at their eyes, it is about concentrating on the caller, not on other distractions or your screen. If you're looking at a computer screen your mind is distracted by the information you're looking at.

Consider what is said

As mentioned previously, 55% of a message is received through our body language, 38% through our tone of voice, leaving only 7% of the message being conveyed through what is said. However, that isn't an excuse to neglect what you say as an organisation.

We often get into bad habits and pick up jargon or phrases that don't have the desired impact. For example, I hear the expressions 'no worries' or 'no problem' often in response to requests made by customers or when a customer has thanked a member of staff. If we break down the two words, they both have a negative connotation: 'no' is negative, 'worries' or 'problem' is negative. If we are communicating with someone whose English is limited, they may misunderstand—are you telling me 'no', or is there 'a problem'? Alternatively, what should be said in response to a request is 'Certainly, yes', or in response to a thank you, 'You're welcome' or 'It's my pleasure'. When the body language that is seen by the customer complements the words, this leaves the recipient with a sense of positivity.

There will be times when the answer is 'no', yet how this is explained to the customer requires some consideration. All colleagues must remember the intention of wanting the customer to return. To think about a long-term relationship rather than the moment.

CASE STUDY

I recently visited our local Post Office to purchase a non-bendy A4 envelope. I was told, 'We don't have any.' This was coupled with a body language of gazing blankly at me. I was stunned by the response. A few moments seemed to pass before I explained what I was trying to do, and did they have anything that might meet that need? No solution was provided. I didn't purchase anything.

On reflection from this, consider:
- As a customer, have you ever experience these blank looks as you've wanted to purchase something? How does this leave you feeling? What do you think?
- Would you return to use this Post Office's services?
- What would you have done as a staff member?

Before thinking about your business, here are a few of my thoughts:
- I think (in this moment) this person was rude and not at all interested in looking after their customers.
- I have the impression they are transactional. They carry out the simple requests, however anything outside of that does not interest them. Their job could quite easily be carried out by a robot. (We're seeing many roles being replaced with automated solutions.)
- This person had no desire to use their brain to seek possible solutions for my request.
- No apology was given as my expectation wasn't met. I think my expectation to buy an envelope from the Post Office wasn't unreasonable. (You might have a different perspective!)
- Ideally this person could have responded with, 'I'm sorry, we don't stock what you're looking for. May I show you what we do have to see if these might be suitable?' Had they not been suitable, they might have been able to suggest where I could find them.
- Preferably, do not respond with 'no'. Always share with your customers what 'we can do.'

Thinking about your business:
- How do your team respond to a customer's request if/when they don't have the product or service they are looking for?
- Do they have sufficient product knowledge to be able to support the customer to find a suitable alternative or reference for where they can get what they want?

The written word: what is heard?

There are so many examples of what is being said not quite hitting the mark. What do your customers hear via the written word, whether this is from notices, in emails or even letters?

Notices are often displayed in establishments where refurbishment or maintenance is taking place stating 'We're sorry for the inconvenience.' While it is good that they acknowledge it is an inconvenience, I'm not sure why they apologise. This might be controversial, however. My take on this is that they should say that they want to make this right for their customers in the future and it is a temporary inconvenience to make their next experience exceptional. Maybe it would be better to change the message to something along the lines of 'Thank you for your patience as we go through this period of change. We look forward to seeing you again in our new look premises'.

I often read 'Please do not hesitate to contact me' at the end of emails. It leaves me thinking 'Hesitate? Why would I hesitate? Now you've said that, I think I'm hesitating!' Instead, state what you want the person receiving the message to do. It would read like this: 'Please contact me if you have any questions.' Simple.

Notices and signs are all very good. However, there is nothing like things being explained and brought to life for you personally in a way that you understand. Many organisations think displaying a notice will ensure all customers hear the message. In reality, they don't. What you are doing is putting the responsibility on the customer to read everything. This is passing the buck, putting the blame on the customer: 'There's a sign there, didn't you see it?' or 'It's written there in the small print.' I think it's lazy and not at all customer focused. It is so much better when things are talked through with the customer; it also gives you the opportunity to check what the customer has understood. This builds confidence for your customer and makes a difference. To provide both an explanation and written information would be an exceptional outcome.

Many professional services are guilty of talking in their own specific way, which is often full of jargon that is not understood by their customers. You being the professional is why your services are needed by the consumer. However, I think this is often forgotten. For example, many accountants talk 'accountant language' that is not understood by their clients; it needs to be translated so the customer understands. This is also the case in banks, solicitors, estate agents, engineers, builders, plumbers, car mechanics, doctors, nurses and the list continues. Overall, I believe you need to ask your customer what they have understood and make it easy for them to ask questions without feeling intimidated.

Whilst we're on the subject of professional services, a point that was well made by a friend is what they want to hear is 'sound advice'. This is so true. Solicitors, financial advisors, doctors, mechanics and the rest should speak in a language we understand, with reasons why they believe the advice they are giving is sound and aligned to our specific needs. Organisations who consider their long-term reputation are the ones who want to build trust for the long-term benefit of their clients, not short term. They are the ones who can translate into layman's terms. They are the ones who get repeat business. We as customers like to feel that we have a good understanding of what we're doing or buying. We like to feel calm, confident, clear and have at least a small amount of control.

Your team needs to have the correct knowledge to build trust and confidence with your customers. Whilst they need to have all the relevant information required, are they helpful in meeting the customer's expectations and needs?

Notes

CASE STUDY

I go to a particular department store (this is the same store where I had the great personal shopping experience mentioned earlier) to buy jeans. As we all know, each store or brand of clothing fit to different sizes. I have always been offered help to ensure the jeans I buy are a good fit, which leaves me feeling confident in my purchase. One day, assured that I would get what I needed, I asked for help. I explained that I loved the jeans I was wearing because they fit me well, but I needed a new pair. I asked what brands they had that would give me a similar fit. The assistant came into the cubicle and agreed that the jeans I was wearing were the right size but gave no offer (as I've become used to) of where I could begin to look in the store for something similar. She left the cubicle and so did I. I purchased nothing. This could have been a deal breaker for me to shift stores. I have since been back to see if things have changed completely. I'm pleased to say they were back to their usual helpful and caring selves. They presented me with a number of options that would suit me. I made a purchase.

On reflection from this, consider:
- What do you believe the challenge is with this situation?
- What has the shop assistant done with the information given to her?
- Would you have returned in this case?

Before thinking about your business, here are few of my thoughts:
- Based on the many positive experiences, I gave this store a second chance. Without the track record of positives, I wouldn't have returned.
- It was disappointing.
- A sale was lost on that day. I doubt the CEO or owner would have been pleased with this outcome.
- The tone of voice and body language left me thinking this person's attitude was not appropriate for dealing with customers.
- Had this person not had the time to assist in their normal supportive and caring way, they could have explained this. She could have said in a considered and genuine tone something like: 'Yes, these jeans are the right fitting for you. Normally I'd go and get a selection for you to try, only I have another customer who is waiting for me. The brands that would be suitable would be x, y and z in this size. These are located on this side of the store. I shall come back to you to see how you are getting on as soon as I'm free.'
- I'm pleased that it seems this incident was isolated.

Thinking about your business:
- Are your customers being put off your business, brand or product as the result of one negative interaction with one of your team?
- What can be done in your business to ensure your customers have a consistently positive experience?
- Are you and your team giving a positive message even in a tricky situation?
- How can you ensure you and your team have all the required product knowledge to make it easy for your customers to buy?

Conversations Customers hear

Customers want to hear positive and appropriate conversation within their earshot. This might be directed to them or a conversation with other customers or colleagues. There is nothing worse than hearing staff chatting to each other, with no focus on customers, moaning or bad-mouthing others.

I often hear a one-word sentence in greeting which sounds abrupt! We've all been there when you approach someone in shops, corporate office receptions or banks, and the person behind the counter or desk looks at you and says 'Yes'. I'm wondering 'Where's the sentence?' What do they actually mean by 'yes'? It is rude, giving the impression the customer is intruding or an inconvenience. When having breakfast in hotels, the waiting team often come along and say 'tea or coffee' or 'toast'. It would be wonderful if these could change to 'Good morning, how can I help you?' or 'Would you like tea or coffee this morning?' or 'May I get you something to drink?' or 'Would you like to have brown, granary or white bread for your toast?' I'm sure we're still taught to speak in sentences rather than single words like toddlers. Are people being lazy? This indicates that you can't be bothered to communicate effectively with your customer.

Your team is on stage.
Make sure what is said is aligned to the show you are performing.

A great example of what your customers hear is on some tube stations on the London Underground. Announcements are made from the platform to ensure that passengers are standing behind the yellow lines as trains approach and everyone boards the train safely. It's wonderful when the platform person makes fun and engaging comments, saying things like 'Welcome to Victoria Station. What a great place to be on this sunny morning. Please take care to stand behind the yellow line. Your safety is important to us. We want you to get to work safe and sound and ready for a fabulous day with your colleagues.' They often continue as everyone boards the train, with 'Please move along the carriage or wait for the next train. Your work will wait for you. It's great to see you, have a wonderful day and we look forward to seeing you tomorrow,' or something along these lines. It's amazing the impact this has on the customers. They are smiling, having a little giggle, and it's simply exceptional. This is one person deciding to make a positive impact on their customers. It's a choice. It makes my day—along with a few hundred other people standing on the platform.

What your customers hear other customers say is also important, whether this is in your business or on social media. It influences your new, potential or former customers. Everyone in your business needs to be on board.

What do your customers hear your team saying to each other? There are so many times I've waited whilst these conversations are prioritised over me paying for items or looking for assistance. The subjects vary from TV programmes, moaning about the weather, their journey in, what needs to be done today, the boss or other colleagues. This is wrong. What makes these colleagues think that it is appropriate?

The training of all colleagues is so important.

They need to fully understand the purpose of their role, to be clear about what success looks, sounds and feels like and how they create this for their customers.

CONSIDER WHETHER YOU AND YOUR COLLEAGUES:

- sound positive?
- sound confident, clear, concise and informative?
- sound happy to help?
- respond with information that is aligned to your customer's needs?
- offer solutions to your customers' wants and needs?
- share information with your customers in a way they understand?
- explain relevant information to your customers so they are fully informed? Rather than leaving them to potentially be caught out by the sign they didn't notice or the small print they haven't read? To be exceptional, you'd offer both.

HEAR EXCEPTIONAL CHECKLIST

Walk around your business. Take the time to listen carefully to the sounds and conversations that are within your earshot and make a point of listening to telephone conversations too. Consider the questions below and make a list of the things that you do well.

Hear exceptional service standards:

Website:

Do your customers hear clear, easily understood and positive messages from your website?	Y ☐	N ☐
What music or audio do your customers experience on your website? Is it a good quality? Is it clear and free from tinny sounds?	Y ☐	N ☐
What messages do your customers and potential customers hear from online reviews by your other customers? Do they gain a positive impression of your business?	Y ☐	N ☐

Outside your business:

What do your customers hear as they arrive at your business? Is this aligned to the overall experience you would like them to have?	Y ☐	N ☐

Inside and throughout your business:

Do your customers hear a genuine warm welcome for themselves and other customers?	Y ☐	N ☐
Do your customers hear positive language with each and every interaction they have with a colleague	Y ☐	N ☐
Do your customers hear music that is complementary to the overall style and mood of your business?	Y ☐	N ☐
Do your customers hear positive background noise, free from unwanted banging doors or the clattering of operational activity they don't want to hear? Free from maintenance or engineering noise?	Y ☐	N ☐
Do your customers hear other customers complimenting the team and your business?	Y ☐	N ☐
Do you and your colleagues sound confident, clear, concise and informative?	Y ☐	N ☐

Do you and your colleagues respond with information that is aligned to your customer's needs? — Y ☐ N ☐

Do you and your colleagues explain relevant information to your customers, so they are fully informed? Rather than leaving them to potentially be caught out by the sign they didn't notice or the small print they haven't read? To be exceptional, you'd offer both. — Y ☐ N ☐

Do your customers hear your colleagues engaging in friendly and appropriate conversation with them and other customers? — Y ☐ N ☐

Do your customers hear your colleagues explore solutions to their needs? — Y ☐ N ☐

Do your customers hear what the colleague has understood from their expectations? — Y ☐ N ☐

Do your customers hear all colleagues greeting or acknowledging them throughout the whole of the business? — Y ☐ N ☐

Do your customers hear full sentences that make sense? — Y ☐ N ☐

Do your customers hear clear and succinct information they need to be aware of, in a way they understand? — Y ☐ N ☐

Do you and your team have an agreed greeting when you answer the phone that showcases your business as you'd like? — Y ☐ N ☐

Do your customers' calls get answered within your standard timescales? — Y ☐ N ☐

Do your customers speak to your colleagues on the phone with no annoying background noises that may distract them from the conversation? — Y ☐ N ☐

Do you and your colleagues give all customers on the phone their undivided attention? Focusing only on the caller? — Y ☐ N ☐

Are all messages that are taken from your customers responded to as you'd like? — Y ☐ N ☐

Which of these do you already do consistently?

Celebrate what you notice you and your team do well. Encourage them to maintain this consistently. As mentioned in the last chapter, if you are leading a team, let them know what they do well, with the intention of creating a feel-good factor and continued great performance. If you are considering your own performance, congratulate yourself and feel proud of what you already do well and continue to do it.

Select the two service standards you want to upgrade or improve within your business and note them here:

1.

2.

Add the two you would like to add to the *Service Standards Checklist* you started in the 'see' chapter. Share your thoughts with your colleagues, and gain their thoughts and insights. Start assessing how you are doing. Here's what it will look like as you assess the reality within your business:

	SERVICE STANDARDS CHECKLIST	YES/ NO
1	**Does the entrance have an attractive curb appeal?** *(See)*	No
	What did you observe/notice? Weeds around the edge of the building and in the gutter in front of our premises. The windows were smeared and there were weeds next to the business signage.	
2	**Are all colleagues looking clean, smart and well presented?** *(See)*	Yes
	What did you observe/notice? Jane and Richard in clean company uniform. Ironed shirts and no stains.	
3	**Do your customers hear positive background music and noise? i.e. no slamming doors, maintenance or clattering from the team?** *(Hear)*	No
	What did you observe/notice? The door going into the admin office bangs each time it closes.	
4	**Are all colleagues looking clean, smart and well presented?** *(Hear)*	Yes
	What did you observe/notice? Sandy greeted the customer with 'Mr Palmer, how are you today?'	

Remember, what is said in your business is not necessarily what is heard by your customers.

Acoustics, background music, what your customers overhear your team say, how clear your message is and using the correct tone, especially whilst on the phone, are all so important when creating a good customer experience. Also, they are fundamental to ensure you get your message across in the best possible way. Consider whether the words you use are exactly what you want to say. Be clear and concise.

We're now going to move on to the next sense which can be perceived as so subtle it's not worth considering. However, it really does make a big difference... smell.

Notes

WHAT OUR CUSTOMERS WANT TO SMELL

S mell seems to be one of the most evocative senses. An aroma of lavender can transport you back to fun family times visiting grandparents, whereas catching a whiff of stewed cabbage may remind you of school dinners.

This is why what your customers smell within your business matters. Of course, some people have a much-heightened sense of smell than others and people's tastes vary considerably. However, there are some basic factors you have to take into account.

CONSIDER:
- Is it your intention to have a distinctive smell associated with your business?
- What overall experience do you want for your customer, in particular considering scent?
- Does the environment complement this experience?
- What do you smell in your business at the moment?
- Consider all areas of the business. What do you want your customers to smell as they step into your business that entices them in? When they are in your business, does what they smell confirm that they made the right decision?
- Do back office spaces smell good, or when that door to the back office is open does the front office get a blast of stale odours?
- Are you missing a trick if you ignore this sensitive (for some) sense?

When you want to be exceptional, this is a great opportunity as so many don't even think about it until they get a whiff of unpleasant odours.

Here's an example to bring this alive. It's a hotel example—no surprise there then!

CASE STUDY

In a fabulous hotel, the Christmas decorations had just been put up and they looked stunning, yet there was no aroma that complemented the decorations, leaving it feeling a bit flat and lacking in atmosphere. Candles with cinnamon tones were placed amongst the central display. It made a huge difference and brought the whole experience alive.

On reflection from this, consider:
- What difference would adding the seasonal candles make to a customer's first impression of the display?
- What would your impression have been of this wonderful display without any complementing aromas?

Before thinking about your business, here are few of my thoughts:
- This small addition linked sight with smell and made a big impact. The customer would be more likely to want to stay in the festive area, maybe have some seasonal drinks, rather than leave to celebrate elsewhere.
- All our senses are connected and need to work together to create an experience. When you also add sound with appropriate Christmas music, along with friendly conversation, the impact is magical.

Thinking about your business:
- What is the ambience that you want in your premises?
- Which sense might not be getting the attention it needs in order to create the ideal customer experience?
- What scent may enhance your customer experience?

Smelly premises

Exceptional places give the aromas within their establishments careful thought to ensure that their customers have the ultimate experience. This is often apparent in luxurious or mid-range spas and hotels to give them the luxury feel. I don't know what that gorgeous spa scent is, but for me it is synonymous with relaxation, being pampered and cared for. There's a hotel in London I've visited a few times, and I want to stand in the lobby all day. It smells gorgeous. Not overpowering or toxic, just at the right level.

Aromas can make the experience memorable.

There are, of course, those wonderful fresh smells that lead you to want to buy, such as freshly baked bread, cakes or freshly ground coffee. These are all very tempting, and I'm sure people buy more based on these fabulous smells. These techniques are even used for the sale of property. There are other examples where the scent may lead to sales, the obvious one being flower shops or clothing shops.

There is a branded high street clothing store who clearly pays attention to the whole customer experience. Because they have decided to set the atmosphere with very low lighting, the customer's sense of smell is heightened and so they ensure that the shops smell wonderful. They sell their own fragrances too, and I bet they are bestsellers. They add to the whole experience by having attractive personnel greeting you at the door. This is an example of a company knowing their customer. I am pretty sure this wouldn't work in a clothes store whose main customer base is over 60!

One of my favourite stores sell beautiful linen, gorgeous gifts, candles and clothing. The scent is amazing. It makes me want to recreate the whole experience in my home. There are some charismatic book shops which have an old smell attached to them, giving the impression of old and valued books where people have studied and valued them. Bedding shops often have the scent of clean linen permeating the store.

What is it you are selling and what aromas will encourage people to buy and feel connected to your business?

The timing of these aromas is also important. For example, bacon sandwiches are tempting in the morning, yet off-putting in the evening; the smell of beer & wine in the morning is often not welcome, yet in the evening, an enticing draw.

However, there are many eating and drinking establishments that smell stale or musty, many that reek of fatty odours or stale beer, which is so unpleasant. As soon I get a whiff of these smells, I'm out. It gives the customer the impression of somewhere that is unclean and unhygienic. People don't necessarily need to see the cleanliness or state of your business, as they make their assessment on smell alone. Well I do, and I'm sure there are many like me.

You know if food is fresh or stale by its smell. Stale food or stale air, both are unappealing. There are businesses that smell musty, closed, and as though fresh air has not been let in for months or even years. It's unhealthy and not welcoming. The customer wonders what is causing the smells, which leads to them to a conclusion that the property is not well maintained. If there is a musty smell, this indicates damp or rot to me. It needs fixing!

We talked about toilets in the 'See' chapter, and this is the time to visit the loo again! It only takes one customer to create an unwanted aroma, this necessary evil, but what are you doing to get rid of it when it happens? When I see windows that are open or can be opened in the loo, it makes me smile. I'm strange like that!

It is not only in the toilet area where fresh air is important. I am a big advocate of bringing fresh air into a building. Not only is it healthy, it gives an impression of cleanliness and life. When possible, open windows and adjoining doors to allow for air circulation—maybe before your clients arrive. Rooms that have been shut off, without fail, tend to be musty and stale. Fresh plants and flowers can assist with this as they absorb odours from the air, replacing them with good old oxygen. Of course, the water in the flowers and the health of the plants need to be maintained otherwise they create unwanted smells too!

Bleach is another distinctive and overpowering smell. When it is strong, I have the impression that it is used to cover up dirt and smells. The ultimate loo experience would be either neutral (fresh and airy) or a subtle pleasant fragrance.

There are some great businesses out there that specialise in these things. Here are a couple that I have found, who might be able to assist you.

Aromaco.co.uk

It is interesting what is stated on their website:
- *Research has shown that of the five senses, smell is the sense most linked to our emotional recollection. So, when linked to a product, it can reap dividends.*
- *Studies show that 75% of emotions are triggered by smell which is linked to pleasure, well-being and memory.*

Also Ecoscent.co.uk

Noted on their website:

Scent Marketing is the act of engaging your customer through the subtle presentation of sensory elements into the environment—specifically, by targeting their sense of smell and creating pleasant surroundings.

When a business presents a sensory experience, which engages their customers' olfactory senses, it can evoke a favourable subconscious reaction which helps reinforce positive brand associations.

They state that they offer scents for all differing types of business, such as hotels, retail, leisure, gym, home and office.

I think it's worth getting the experts in to assist.

CONSIDER:

- Are your premises thoroughly aired?
- Do you have extractor fans that carry odours to other areas of your business that might impact on your customers or team?
- Are all your extractors fans clean and working effectively? Extractor fans that are full of dust and grime are not working effectively.
- Are you creating your desired atmosphere/aroma within your business?
- Are your premises well maintained? Free from musty odours?
- Do you fix the drains, mould, etc., by getting to the root of the problem, enabling you to build a positive experience for everyone?
- Do your premises smell clean, fresh and inviting?

Smelly people

Moving on to the people in your business. Are they aligned and complementing the customer experience? These personal subjects are difficult to address but they are important when you are striving to ensure that your customers have the ultimate experience. It can be embarrassing to discuss basic hygiene with people in your team or if they mention this to you about another team member...or even yourself! However, it is necessary to have these discussions when needed. Good body odour is critical; if you or your team can smell body odours or bad breath then so can your customers. Again, it's all about what experience you want your customers to have.

CASE STUDY

During my time working in hotels there have been several occasions when I have been asked to speak to a colleague about their stale and off-putting body odour. There was one particular time that sticks in my mind. I had been facilitating a programme. It was coffee break and everyone left the room, apart from two guys. They were laughing. I asked what was so funny and I was concerned when they told me it was about a female colleague in the group who had a problem with sweat odours. I would not like to have been her and have people behaving like this behind my back. I asked to catch up with her privately before the session continued. She went to shower, change and to do whatever she needed to do.

On reflection from this, consider:
- What would you have done if you had been me?
- How do you think the two guys could have handled this, instead of laughing at their colleague?

Before thinking about your business, here are a few of my thoughts:
- It is important that all colleagues are fully aware of self-care. Whilst this did form part of the initial training given, some people's understanding differs from the expectation.
- People can be cruel. I have always been happy to talk to people about these personal issues as I'd rather someone tell me so I can do something about it. It would be awful to have people talking behind my back. I have noticed that people would rather talk behind people's back than address them privately and considerately.
- How long had this person endured this personal issue and how many customers had noticed? This person was representing the company and they could quite easily be the only person an individual customer had interacted with.
- Any one colleague is representing the whole of your workforce, including you and 'the big cheese'.
- Personal hygiene might be perceived as common sense. However, as Ghandi quoted, 'Common sense is not common.'

Thinking about your business:
- Are you and your team clear about personal hygiene standards and expectations?
- How will you ensure these standards and expectations are met?
- Who would be the right person to approach any issues? Ensuring anyone is spoken to in private in the most considerate and dignified way?

In some businesses where the team is active, odours are more likely. Does your team have the opportunity to freshen up mid shift to ensure they are customer ready? As when dealing with unpleasant smells in the environment, the key is to wash, not to cover up odour with overpowering deodorants, perfumes or aftershaves.

A past colleague left a stench of her strong perfume when she left the room. I used to say, 'Has Maureen just been in here?' When people would ask how I knew, I always found it tricky to reply without saying 'I can smell her!' A hint of pleasant aroma is lovely, yet so much that you can taste, not so lovely.

Many teams have an opportunity to take a break, which often includes having a cigarette. I know this is a personal choice, however the odour does stay with you, whether you're the one smoking or you are in the company of smokers. The number of times I have asked someone, 'Have you just had a cigarette?' and they've been curious as to how I knew. Well, it was blooming obvious; the smell that is carried is awful.

A friend used to comment about her high-end hairdresser who used to chew gum after having a cigarette. He didn't realise how unpleasant it was to have him cutting and styling her hair, with his hands smelling of nicotine so close to her nose and face. Not good. She was paying premium price for the privilege too.

Getting the balance right is crucial;
a pleasant scent without being overwhelming

If you are faced with having to highlight a personal odour issue, here are some handy hints you might find helpful:

- Ensure you catch them in private, where others cannot overhear.
- Explain that you have a tricky situation that you wish to share directly with them, rather than it escalating any further.
- Assure them that this conversation is in confidence and will not be shared with anyone else. (Make sure you don't share it with anyone else.)
- Explain that you have noticed body odour coming from them, that you want to highlight this with them so that they have the opportunity to address it.
- Leave the conversation as that. Reassure them that you will not mention this again unless necessary, in which case you will speak directly with them.

- Do you and your team appreciate the importance of good personal hygiene?
- What perception do you have of your business, based on the cleanliness of each individual within your team? Does this make you feel proud? Do you need to support and guide them to play their important part within your team and business?

To summarise smells

There are many ways to consider using scent to build an exceptional experience. In exceptional organisations, they spray their signature aroma onto the stationery they send to their customers. WOW! What a first impression!

There is so much that can be done to create a truly exceptional experience, and the basics of good cleanliness is the foundation of it all. With cleanliness, you can then take the next steps to create complementary smells to encourage your customers to return. Consider creating different aromas in different areas of your business. Use diffusers, or candles where it's safe to do so. This all depends on what ambience you are striving to create.

Notes

SMELL EXCEPTIONAL CHECKLIST

Take a walk around your business. Take the time to notice the scents of the environment and of your team. Consider these questions and make a list of the positive things you notice.

Smell exceptional service standards:

Fresh people

Do you and your team have fresh breath?	Y ☐	N ☐
Do you and your team have a fresh, clean body and clean hair? Free from nicotine, drugs or stale food or body odour?	Y ☐	N ☐
Do you and your team's clothes smell fresh? Free from nicotine, drugs or stale food or body odour?	Y ☐	N ☐
Do you and your team wear subtle and understated deodorants, perfume or aftershave which is not overpowering?	Y ☐	N ☐

Fresh premises

Are your premises fresh and thoroughly aired?	Y ☐	Y ☐
Are your premises free from the smell of overpowering cleaning products, bleach, etc.?	Y ☐	N ☐
Are your plants and flowers smelling fresh and healthy? Do the flowers have fresh water?	Y ☐	N ☐
Do you have delightful aromas that entice your customers to buy your products? Such as fresh bread, coffee, relaxing spa scents.	Y ☐	N ☐
Are your toilets facilities aired?	Y ☐	N ☐
Are your toilets free from overpowering cleaning product odours?	Y ☐	N ☐
Are all your extractor fans clean and working effectively?	Y ☐	N ☐
Are your premises free from poor maintenance odours?	Y ☐	N ☐
Are your premises free from any musty, mould or stale food smells?	Y ☐	N ☐
Are you premises promoting positive food aromas at the appropriate time of the day? e.g. fresh bread, fresh coffee, etc.	Y ☐	N ☐
Are you premises free from the smell of stale fat or grease?	Y ☐	N ☐
Are you using aromas to enhance your customer experience?	Y ☐	N ☐

Which of these do you already do consistently?

Celebrate what you notice you and your team do well. Encourage them to maintain this consistently. Share what you have noticed with your team, so they are likely to continue to create that feel-good factor and high standards.

Select the two service standards you want to upgrade or improve within your business and note them here:

1.

2.

Add the two points you have chosen to your checklist.

SERVICE STANDARDS CHECKLIST		YES/ NO
1	**Does the entrance have an attractive curb appeal?** *(See)*	No
	What did you observe/notice? Weeds around the edge of the building and in the gutter in front of our premises. The windows were smeared and there were weeds next to the business signage.	
2	**Are all colleagues looking clean, smart and well presented?** *(See)*	Yes
	What did you observe/notice? Jane and Richard in clean company uniform. Ironed shirts and no stains.	
3	**Do your customers hear positive background music and noise? i.e. no slamming doors, maintenance or clattering from the team?** *(Hear)*	No
	What did you observe/notice? The door going into the admin office bangs each time it closes.	

SERVICE STANDARDS CHECKLIST		YES/NO
4	**Are all the team engaging with customers using positive language?** *(Hear)*	Yes
	What did you observe/notice? Sandy greeted the customer with 'Mr Palmer, how are you today?'	
5	**Do your premises smell fresh and aired?** *(Smell)*	Yes
	What did you observe/notice? No unpleasant odours. Could potentially feel more aired.	
6	**Do all your toilet facilities smell fresh and aired?** *(Smell)*	No
	What did you observe/notice? A strong smell of chemicals in the loos.	

Appropriate scent and smells can enhance your customer experience. Yet awful odours can be off-putting and potentially be detrimental to your business. It has to be appropriate for the type of business and the time of day and not overwhelming.

This sense complements our next chapter, where we explore taste.

5

WHAT OUR CUSTOMERS WANT TO TASTE

T his sense is particularly important in eateries and drinking holes for obvious reasons. However, it also has a personal taste connotation too. We shall look at both.

If your business doesn't serve food or drink in any form (including a cup of tea or a glass of water or even a mint), skip to the second half of the chapter where we talk about personal taste.

Food and Drink

Let us start with the basics.

- Do your customers talk about the fresh products they associate with your business and their amazing taste?
- Are you proud of the food and drink you serve or sell?
- Is the food and drink you serve perceived by your customer as good value for money?
- What is it your customers want or need from you?

What your customers want is
fresh food that is safe to eat.

I think this is so basic, yet there are many places that don't seem to get this right. These vary from small take-away establishments to fine dining, which are seen to be exclusive restaurants.

So, first things first—food hygiene. When I read in the news about food poisoning, it makes my skin crawl. This is your reputation. When you open your doors to serve food to the public they are trusting that you have all the right processes and procedures in place to ensure that food tastes good and is fit for human consumption.

Everything we have talked about in this book is about building trust and getting the basics in place. They say that 'trust takes years to build, seconds to break and forever to repair.' It is important that we make the right call when it comes to our customers' well-being and health. There is a huge amount of legislation around this and it is there to protect us all as consumers. We need to take it seriously. The hygiene scores on the doors have already been mentioned. A hygiene rating of five fills me with confidence, whereas anything lower leaves me wondering what is missing. Or what has been overlooked?

This isn't just the case for businesses where food is the main product. There are many examples of clothes boutiques, banks, car showrooms, etc., where a cup of coffee (or even champagne in some high-end jewellery shops) is served to help you feel comfortable and want to stay and buy. Many shops and businesses offer a bowl of sweets at the till for customers to help themselves. In these instances, it is just as important that the beverage and food served is edible and even enjoyable. For example, in a wedding boutique where champagne is served to enhance the experience, if the champagne is flat and warm, then the purpose is lost. It's even the simple things, like a bowl of mints in estate agents that are covered in dust. Coffee that is bitter and cold. If you are going to do something, do it well. Give the attention it needs to make the positive impact you intended.

Let's assume you have all the correct legislation in place to ensure safety for everyone. With this all adhered to and all checks in place, now let's consider the experience for your customers and what your business is all about.

Food and drink needs to be what it is supposed to be: hot food and drink is hot, and cold food and drink is cold. You'd think this was obvious, yet what we experience as consumers is often 'warm' or 'tepid', or even the opposite, with hot being cold. This is rubbish!

Tasty or not?

There are so many examples I can give. For me, there is nothing like a well-made gin and tonic: cold glass full of ice, carefully chosen gin and tonic, complete with fresh garnish—delicious! Yet so often it is served in a warm glass (straight from the glass washer), one or two pieces of ice and the rest of the ingredients shoved in. It's just not the same. I wonder if we have ice shortages at times! Likewise with beer: cold glass, cold beer is an amazing experience, leaving you wanting another. Yet those warm glasses seem to be in abundance everywhere. I don't understand why bars and restaurants can't get it right. Champagne and white wines are other examples—and believe me, I've done a lot of sampling, purely for research, you understand!

Hot drinks are the same. I don't generally order tea when I'm out and about, as it doesn't seem to be hot by the time it is served. When tea is served in a teapot, the teapot should be warmed with boiling water to retain the heat in the teapot and enhance the tea experience. Tea is made from boiling water, not just-off-the-boil water. The containers the hot drinks are served in should be warm; I guess straight from the dishwashers works in this case.

Again, food is exactly the same: hot food is to be served on hot plates to retain its heat, cold on cold. I've often experienced buffets with the plates offered being warm—lettuce placed on a warm surface is not pleasant as it's supposed to be a fresh, crisp salad. Lukewarm food is not good either, especially for high-risk foods such as chicken. Make sure the food is served at the correct temperature direct to your customers.

The freshness of food is important too. If doesn't look fresh, it's likely that it's not. Lettuce is again a good example. I'm not sure why lettuce that is limp with brown edges is seen as being acceptable to serve or sell to customers.

I realise that none of this is simple to do, as it requires careful ordering to ensure you maximise on the small window for when food is at its best. Nobody said that any of this would be easy. However, when it's done right, your business will flourish and grow. It is worth considering having a smaller range of products and making sure you do them perfectly. This allows you to master stock control.

Better to do a small number of things well than a large selection which is not as good and not as fresh, leading to waste and dissatisfied customers.

> There's a small café and gift shop in the Northern Quarter in Manchester, with emphasis on the small. In my opinion, it's fabulous. The look and feel of the premises is rustic. Yet what they sell is unique, offering items that you don't generally get to see in many other shops. The food and drinks are homemade and delicious, yet there's not a huge range of products to buy. In my opinion, it is small and perfectly formed. It's always busy and in good taste.

The identity of your business will determine what food you serve. For example, are your customers buying food to meet a hunger need or do they desire a dining experience?

Be clear about what you are selling and to whom.

When I dine out, it will normally be to catch up with family or friends. I'm usually so engrossed in the conversation that I don't give the food or drink I'm consuming much notice, unless it's awful. (Apologies to all the fabulous chefs I've worked with.) The food has to be exceptional for me to really notice its flavour. A few experiences that really stand out in my mind are Rick Stein's fish restaurant in Padstow and Raymond Blanc's Le Manoir aux Quat Saison. Amazing! Everything was delicious. The chefs at these establishments take huge pride in their art and ensure their teams do too. The prices they charge are worth every penny—and they're not cheap!

There's another super example of exceptional food—a certain city centre breakfast butty stand I used to frequent. Whilst I was working in London, we'd treat ourselves on a Friday morning. The stand was an old taxi rank. It had a hatch where you'd be served and the smell would get your mouth watering in anticipation for your order—fresh bacon cooking (no stale fat smells that turn your stomach). The facilities looked immaculate. When we'd return to the office, there'd be silence as we savoured every mouthful of delicious, thick and crispy bacon on a fresh soft roll. There was always a queue for their breakfasts. Hugely successful and again worth every penny. It's making me hungry just writing about it!

Consistency is everything if you want to build a legacy as the place to go and you want to rely on local repeat business.

CASE STUDY

An international department store that hosts a popular food hall found in most towns and cities is my 'go to' place for a quick sandwich at lunch (take note, speed is important to me in this circumstance). There is a generous filling, kept at the right temperate, and it is tasty and satisfying. It's normally quick and easy to buy. Although there's the odd occasion when it's not quite as fresh as the previous visit; the bread may be a little dry. My last few visits have been disappointing. I have since changed my lunch plans to a store who also offer a more efficient service.

On reflection from this, consider:
- What detail needs to be considered for this company to get it right?
- Who is letting the organisation down?

Before thinking about your business, here are few of my thoughts:
- It is the small things that really matter.
- Fresh bread is critical to an enjoyable sandwich.
- Whoever is preparing the sandwiches is playing an important role in the overall experience for the customer.
- The basic need for me is to eat a quick lunch. Yet I want it to be fresh and taste good.
- I don't want to eat stale food.
- I believe people are becoming more conscientious about what they eat. If you rely on people accepting average or mediocre food, I think you will eventually lose your customers.
- Whilst this is not an exclusive 'dining' experience, there is no reason for it to be poor.
- Fresh food every time is the basic need and expectation of your customers.

Thinking about your business:
- What food do you sell or serve? Is it fresh?
- Do you and your colleagues know what is acceptable to sell and serve to your customers? And what is not?
- Is there clear evidence that you have good stock rotation practices in place? Your customers notice these things. This will prove that you want to ensure all your customers get fresh products—all the time.
- Do your suppliers understand your need for fresh produce?
- Do you have a good relationship with your suppliers to ensure you can offer a consistently fresh product that your customers love?

Again, the difficulty is to ensure that the experience people have is consistent. It would be awful if I were to go back to the fabulous eateries I've just mentioned and be disappointed. I'd be upset if you went—especially on my advice—and had a bad experience. What would that say about my recommendation? Although we could always put it down to our own unique personal taste!

This leads me on to consider the complex, unique taste of your customers. This is a difficult one!

Knowing your customers

The choice of food and drink that you offer is fundamental to the success of your business.

CONSIDER:

- Who is your ideal customer?
- Does the food and drink you offer appeal to your customers or does it appeal to you, the person purchasing your food and drink products, or your chef?
- What are the seasonal foods that you might want to consider?
- What are the latest health trends that might influence the food or drink you sell or serve?
- What is the latest trendy dish, product or high-profile celebrity 'thing' to eat or drink?
- Do your customers prefer to have vegan, vegetarian, dairy-free, sugar-free, gluten-free, and/or allergen-free options?
- Do your customers want to see locally produced products?
- What's the lasted film or TV cookery show that might influence the food your customers may want to taste?
- What research will you consider so that you can keep up with the eating and drinking habits of your customers?
- Maybe ask your customers for some feedback so you can meet their expectations.

Having worked in the hospitality industry for over 30 years, I have met many chefs. Most of them have a huge passion for food and are highly skilled in their role (which I love and admire about them). There are some who design menus around their knowledge and likes, to show off their expertise, which is fabulous. However, I think some of them might forget that this is all about the customer. Do their customers like these fancy items on the menu, those things on the menu that no-one recognises or actually wants to eat? Are food stores filled with the food the proprietor likes, rather than what their customers like?

CASE STUDY

I might be showing my ignorance here, I know, but I have the urge to share my experience at a posh banqueting dinner I once attended. We had pigeon as our starter; it was awful—tough, dry and tasted terrible. Who likes pigeon? Whilst I know there will be people out there who do, I doubt the majority of the people in that room of 300 people did. I would like to have seen all the plates that were cleared from that banquet and see how much meat was not eaten—not that there's much on a pigeon!

On reflection from this, consider:
- Would you have enjoyed pigeon? (I'd love to do a survey of everyone who reads this book to see how many people would have enjoyed it, to establish if I have the right perception or not.)
- What would have been more suitable?

Before thinking about your business, here are few of my thoughts:
- Serve what most people in the room love and enjoy. Be clear about the outcome you are striving to achieve. I'd want everyone raving about how delicious the food was.
- Keep it simple, yet exceptional, and the best your customers have ever tasted.
- I think this was an expensive waste. I had a wasted exceptional taste experience. A waste of food. A wasted opportunity for the hotel to build on its reputation.
- I think this chef wanted to 'show off' or expected everyone to like what they did.

Thinking about your business:
- What dishes or drinks do you offer? Are there any you notice that are not often chosen by your customers? Does this indicate that perhaps you might remove it from your business?
- Do you find some dishes or drinks are often returned and end up in the bin? What waste have you noticed?
- From the waste you notice that is left by your customers, what do you think your customers are saying to other people about what they have left? What is the unseen or unknown cost of this waste?
- What are you doing to make sure every dish and drink sold and served is delicious? How does this impact on the whole experience your customers have? What positive impact does this have on your business?
- Are your food and drink products simple yet exceptional?
- What will you do to ensure the right dishes, food products and drinks are being offered to your customers?

There is no better advert than demonstrating your faith in your product. There are food stores that have taster stands, which give the customers the opportunity to taste certain products. I avoid them as I know I'll end up buying them, but most people flock to them. This says to me 'We are proud of this product and we're sure you will like it.' Of course, this is what they want you to do—buy the product. This reminds me of Gordon Ramsey, in his TV show *Ramsey's Kitchen Nightmares,* when he goes into the community to 'showcase' and taste some dishes of the restaurant he's trying to promote and get back on its feet. He gets feedback from the people he meets and he can then gauge whether it will be a hit or not. This process usually results in queues of people wanting a table when the restaurant reopens!

I recently met a friend for lunch. We were chatting away and the waiter came over a few times to see if we were ready to order. We weren't—too busy chatting! However, we decided to choose so we could then carry on with our conversation. It all went quiet for a while as we studied the menu. Eventually, I said I didn't know what to order as there was nothing that took my fancy. There was one item that would be 'all right', which is the one that we both ordered. Not good. This is a new restaurant, gorgeous furnishings, clean and impressive, in a brilliant location. I'm not a fussy person when it comes to food so to have only one item on the menu which appealed to me was pretty hopeless! I won't be going back to eat as there's nothing to my taste, but maybe I'd return for a drink.

It's so important to know what your customers' tastes are. Are you clear about the products you are selling and does it match the tastes of who you are selling them to?

Personal taste

This leads us into the personal taste in design, look and feel for the environment.

The surroundings within your business has a massive impact on the customer experience. As already mentioned, it has to be clean and smell fresh, but also has to be in the taste of your ideal customer. There is no point having gold leaf wallpaper, fine bone china teacups and plush carpets if your business is located in the countryside, where your main clientele is likely to be dog walkers. China mugs, stone flooring and stone walls would be more appropriate, with freshwater bowls for the dogs. It's important to create the environment where your ideal customers feel welcomed and comfortable.

Does your business have a clear identity that is aligned to your ideal customer? This is what we talked about in Chapter 1—Who is your customer?

CONSIDER:

- Is your business attracting people who like traditional, rustic, trendy, retro, gothic, light, bright, dark, dull or something else?
- Do your customers come to your business for comfort, luxury or is their visit purely functional?
- Are you located by the sea with surfing clients? What environment would suit them best?
- Are you located in a city with business clients? What environment would best suit them?
- Are you located out of town with a mixed client base, with old, young, and children all forming your client base? What environment would best suit them?
- Do your customers want minimalistic or flamboyant and ornate?
- Do you have a theme that is obvious or are you trying a little of everything, which might be confusing for your customer?
- Is the environment tempting for your customers to want to call in?

Ask yourself whether it is your taste or the taste of the majority. Have you ever watched *The Hotel Inspector*, where Alex Polizzi visits failing hotels, bed and breakfasts, self-catering places, etc.? One of the common threads with these places is the owner like their ornaments, decorations or food, yet these are perceived by most people as bad taste. Often these places having mixed messages which are not aligned to one theme, look and feel, or taste. These things need to flow and give the customers a reassurance that your business suits their taste and has a clear identity. This is the same principle as the food you serve—simple yet done well. The whole look and taste need to work together with a clear style. Not trying to be all things to all men (people).

Whilst exploring Bilbao on a mini break, we discovered a number of bars in one area of the city. They were lively and welcoming, so we investigated, and of course had a drink or two. It was apparent after our tipple that these bars had a certain style, aimed at music and the arts. There were few seats, plenty of standing room, and noticeboards full of advertisements for the next local band who were due to play. My nephew would absolutely love the vibe and taste of these area. However, whilst we enjoyed our evening, we didn't return, as it's simply not us. And that's fine, as it was obviously busy and knew its ideal customer well—it just wasn't us.

CASE STUDY

Sticking with drinking establishments, there's a pub in a local town centre, and about 5-10 years ago it upgraded its interior to appear funkier, with neon lights, open space, pool tables, etc., moving away from the small nooks and intimate seating. Whilst this pub probably did need a refurbishment and may have wanted to attract people to watch the big sporting games, they seemed to have missed a trick. It was labelled as a sports bar; with the new look, they would promote themselves as this. Following the refurbishment, the only time you would see it busy is when a big game was showing. What happened to those people who used to frequent this pub before, as it had a steady clientele? It has now closed. This leaves me feeling sad.

On reflection from this, consider:
- What kind of pub are you attracted to?
- Would you engage with the pub in this example on a non-televised sports day?

Before thinking about your business, here are few of my thoughts:
- Whilst this pub was probably in the need of a refurbishment, I have the impression that they have only thought of the needs of one type of customer.
- The refurbishment must have cost a fair amount of money.
- The customers I believe they were targeting are the people who love sport and enjoy the social atmosphere of being in a pub with like-minded people. Which is great.
- There is also the fact that many people now have access to many sporting channels at home and don't need to watch at the pub.
- It seems this pub targeted only this type of clientele, as outside of these events there were little patronage.
- The intimacy and atmosphere of a traditional pub feel had been lost and didn't meet the taste of other customers, such as small groups of people socialising, couples, locals, etc.
- I have never been inclined to call into these sports bars, yet I love a couple of drinks in a cosy pub with friends.
- The changes that were made could have been balanced with serving excellent food and having alternative seating so that people would still come when sports are not playing. Or did they make enough on sports days to be able to afford to do this? From the fact that they closed soon after, it seems not.

Thinking about your business:
- Do the surroundings of your business meet the needs and expectations of your customers?
- Does the environment fit the taste of differing types of customers so your business can remain buoyant throughout the year, months, weeks, days and time of day?
- Is there a risk that your target market will not be sufficient to make your business viable?
- What might you want to do to ensure your premises are tasteful to your customers?

There have been times when I've stayed in hotels and have thought I'd rather be staying at home. Not a treat at all. Many hotels have stepped up and have invested in their properties so that they are a place where I now stay and feel inspired by the experience. Often these places offer small menus with options that will suit many people, yet the food is simple and tasty. If you know who your customers are, you know their tastes. This makes it easier for you to ensure that your premises meet their expectations.

Is your business somewhere your customers want to be?

Notes

TASTE EXCEPTIONAL CHECKLIST

Walk around your business. Take the time to consider your ideal customer and decide whether your business is aligned to what they'd like. Make note of the food and drink products that sell well versus those that don't. Make a point of tasting one or two food and drink items to ensure they are produced at the standard you want for your customers. Consider these questions and make a list of the things that you do well.

Taste exceptional service standards:

Website:

Would what your customers see on your website appeal to your ideal customer's taste?	Y ☐	N ☐
Does the food you sell look tasty?	Y ☐	N ☐
Do the drinks look appetising?	Y ☐	N ☐

Outside your business:

Is the style of your business meeting the needs and expectations of your ideal customers? Would the design meet their personal taste? Would it entice them into your premises?	Y ☐	N ☐
Does your business have a clear style or theme that is recognisable to your ideal customer?	Y ☐	N ☐

Inside and throughout your business:

Does the environment within your business complement the style and theme that is shown outside?	Y ☐	N ☐
Does your business have a clear image that suits your business location. Is it: Traditional? Rustic? Trendy? Retro? Gothic? Light? Bright? Dark? Dull? Minimalistic? Ornate? Of course...add your own as this list could go on forever.	Y ☐	N ☐
Does the food you sell or serve work well with the theme or style of business?	Y ☐	N ☐
Do the drinks you sell or serve work well with the theme or style of business?	Y ☐	N ☐
Is the food and drink you offer aligned to the tastes of your customers and not the person who buys or produces the products within your business?	Y ☐	N ☐

Are all your food and drink items selling? Do you need to reconsider the items which are not selling?	Y ☐	N ☐
Is the food and drink safe for your customers to eat? Is there good stock rotation?	Y ☐	N ☐
Do you have a high food and drink hygiene score that you are proud of?	Y ☐	N ☐
Is the hot food and drink you sell hot?	Y ☐	N ☐
Is the cold food and drink you sell cold?	Y ☐	N ☐
Is the hot food and drink you serve presented on a hot plate, warmed teapot and warm cup, mug or glass?	Y ☐	N ☐
Is the cold food and drink you serve presented on a cold plate, chilled glass?	Y ☐	N ☐
Does the food taste delicious? Can you identify the flavours?	Y ☐	N ☐
Are the drinks amazing? Can you identify the flavours?	Y ☐	N ☐
Is the food and drink served consistently fresh and tasting good?	Y ☐	N ☐
Are all messages that are taken from your customers responded to as you'd like?	Y ☐	N ☐

Which of these do you already do consistently?

Celebrate what you notice you and your team do well. Encourage them to maintain this consistently. Share what you have noticed with your team, so they are likely to continue to create that feel-good factor and high standard.

Select the two service standards you want to upgrade or improve within your business and note them here:

1.

2.

Add the two points you have chosen to your blank Service Standards Checklist. I think you're getting into the swing of this now!

SERVICE STANDARDS CHECKLIST		YES/NO
1	**Does the entrance have an attractive curb appeal?** *(See)*	No
	What did you observe/notice? Weeds around the edge of the building and in the gutter in front of our premises. The windows were smeared and there were weeds next to the business signage.	
2	**Are all colleagues looking clean, smart and well presented?** *(See)*	Yes
	What did you observe/notice? Jane and Richard in clean company uniform. Ironed shirts and no stains.	
3	**Do your customers hear positive background music and noise? i.e. no slamming doors, maintenance or clattering from the team?** *(Hear)*	No
	What did you observe/notice? The door going into the admin office bangs each time it closes.	
4	**Are all the team engaging with customers using positive language?** *(Hear)*	Yes
	What did you observe/notice? Sandy greeted the customer with 'Mr Palmer, how are you today?'	
5	**Do your premises smell fresh and aired?** *(Smell)*	Yes
	What did you observe/notice? No unpleasant odours. Could potentially feel more aired.	

SERVICE STANDARDS CHECKLIST		YES/ NO
6	**Do all your toilet facilities smell fresh and aired?** *(Smell)*	No
	What did you observe/notice? A strong smell of chemicals in the loos.	
7	**Are all hot foods & drinks service on hot/warm crockery?** *(Taste)*	Yes
	What did you observe/notice? All plates serving hot food felt warm. Napkins available for customers to hold their plates.	
8	**Are all cold foods and drinks served in cold glassware or crockery?** *(Taste)*	No
	What did you observe/notice? A strong smell of chemicals in the loos.	

It's so important to ensure any food or drink you serve is safe for anyone to consume. Ensuring your products are served at the right temperature will support the safety of the product and will enhance the overall experience for your customers. It is worth checking all your product lines to ensure they are selling. Review what your customers are looking for in terms of food and drink.

This is also the case for the style of your business. Is it clear there's a certain look and feel or style? Does this meet your ideal customer's expectations, needs and tastes? Overall, is the experience consistent and does it drive a positive reputation for you and your business? It all matters.

We have one more sense to go, which is a big one.

6

WHAT WE WANT OUR CUSTOMERS **TO FEEL**

How do you feel about exploring our fifth and final sense? It's a huge one to explore as it has two aspects for us to consider. Within this sense you have to consider what you feel when you touch surfaces, what you feel within the atmosphere, and the emotion a customer feels, drawing in all five senses. The emotional aspect is such a big subject I have devoted the next chapter to it.

In this chapter, we shall concentrate on the touch and atmosphere perspective, which I believe is straightforward; however, to reach exceptional levels it needs to be considered carefully.

CONSIDER:

- Are you confident that all surfaces within your business feel clean to your customers?
- Are you confident that the temperature is appropriate for the comfort of your customers?
- Are you confident that the atmosphere is clean and fresh? Rather than humid or damp.
- Are you confident that the areas where your customers sit or stand are free from unwanted drafts?

Feel of quality

Your customers have expectations about the quality and feel of products aligned to the market you are in. For example, when you touch the clothing in designer boutique clothes shops they usually feel rich, smooth and luxurious. That's no surprise at the high price tags they carry! This is important to the customers in this market. What they feel is relevant and needs to be taken into account.

Let's stay with the luxury boutique for a minute and consider all surfaces and what is noticed: the feel of the coffee tables, seating covering, cushions, shelves, receipts, information, brochures, bags for items purchased, floor covering and feeling underfoot. All of which need to feel clean, polished or, if carpeted, to have plenty of bounce or pile. It is totally unacceptable to feel dust or poorly maintained surfaces. It needs to give the impression that no-one else has been there. The boutique is open for the 'one' customer arrival. Whilst there may be many other customers in the shop at one time, the experience would still have a luxurious quality feel, as though you've been waiting for that 'one' customer. In luxury establishments, the paper quality of receipts, business cards and flyers is a great way to assess lavishness: it feels soft, silky and thick. It complements the whole experience they want for their customers.

In hotels with high customer satisfaction, everything the customer touches is thought through. As with the boutique, the furniture, floor covering, fabrics, paper or printed materials are selected precisely to create the ultimate in comfort. In particular, the bed linen and towels ooze extravagance. This defines luxury and is aligned to their customers' expectations.

However, in everyday life, luxury is not something that is necessarily wanted, needed or valued by customers. For example, when I visit the local shop I'm not too bothered if the receipt is printed on silky, soft, thick paper. I simply need a receipt for proof of purchase.

All surfaces

Your business may experience a high volume of customers and ensuring the carpet feels as though it is freshly vacuumed and bouncing underfoot may be virtually impossible. However, clean flooring is a basic standard to ensure a good impression of your business. There is nothing worse than walking into a pub, restaurant, nightclub, coffee shop, shop, or supermarket where you stick to the floor. You can feel it's not clean. You can also 'see' it's unclean, as discussed in the 'See' chapter. Seeing an establishment that is dirty is bad, but when you can't see dirty yet you can 'feel' it, it is as bad, if not even worse. When you walk into a business and can hear and feel your feet sticking to the floor, you know it's dirty.

All our senses link to create an impression of a business.

To bring this to life, here's an example. I recently visited a well-known branded coffee shop. It was looking good, with smart fittings, well-presented food, the floor covering was stunning, the floor tiles were in good repair, no cracks or chips, yet it was slippery. I was wearing rubber-soled shoes; I could easily have slipped. It felt as though oil had been poured over the surface. All I could imagine is whatever they had 'cleaned' the floor with was not clean. What is the point? Or, perhaps they hadn't cleaned the floor at all. In my opinion, if a job is worth doing, it's worth doing well. We know when we are cutting corners.

CONSIDER:

- Is there anything in your business that doesn't get your attention when you consider 'feel'?
- Is there anything that is being covered up? Your customers can sense when things are not done well.
- Do you think you have cleaned the floor because a mop has passed over the surface?
- Is cleanliness important to you and your customers?

When all surfaces feel clean it allows your current customers and potential new customers to feel confident being in your business. This is likely to lead to new customers becoming loyal to you, which is a starting point.

It is not limited to what is felt underfoot. There are so many eating and drinking establishments where the tables or bars feel sticky, wet, grubby or covered in crumbs. It's horrible! It makes the customer feel uncomfortable and unwilling to sit and enjoy the food or drinks, hence they often make a quick exit, not wanting to stay, and the business misses out on them ordering additional drinks, dishes, etc. The main point being that potentially they may never return. I doubt this is the aspiration of business owner or senior leaders. Here's an example of these points being brought to life.

CASE STUDY

I had been looking forward to friends staying with us. We had booked a table at a celebrity chef restaurant. The service was all right, the food good (from what I can remember), however, the lasting memory of this experience was that the tables in the restaurant were tacky, leaving us feeling uncomfortable to rest on them or touch them. It spoilt what should have been a relaxing, indulgent evening. I haven't returned. If my experience had been different I would have been back frequently. I would love to have a local restaurant to frequent for a treat for us and when other friends visit.

On reflection, here are a few of my thoughts:
- I have the impression the cleaning products they use aren't effective in removing grease or sugar.
- When was the last time the tables were cleaned thoroughly?
- Who is responsible for cleaning the tables? Do they understand the purpose of this task and how it has a big impact on the overall experience?
- Has the team been given the right training and guidance? Do they fully understand what good looks and feels like? Have they set their team up for success?

Thinking about your business:
- Are you and your team making sure that any cleaning that takes place within your business has the desired effect for all your customers?
- Are there some details within your business that might be overlooked, which make your customers feel uncomfortable?
- Does the training you and your team receive enable and support them to deliver a great experience every time for your customers?
- If you provide service, yet don't lead, do you feel you have received sufficient training and guidance to provide a great experience for your customers? If not, what will you do to gain this information or guidance?

We can't have a chapter without mentioning the loo! Like it or not, it's where most of your customers are likely to visit. Getting it right is worth it. I can only give reference to this from a woman's perspective. When we visit the loo it's our opportunity to check our make-up, top up on our lipstick, brush our hair and so the list goes on. Therefore, it is important to be able to place our handbags on the side as this spot of pampering takes place. It is not good for all the surfaces to be wet. There are times when the sink area is so wet, if you accidently lean or touch the surface it ends up with your clothing being soaked. Not a good look as you step out. I realise this is an occupational hazard, as at times the taps spray everywhere, and hands drip as they move to the hand dryer or hand drying materials. As mentioned a couple of times throughout the book, none of this is easy. Somehow the toilets need to be monitored to ensure they are clean, tidy and well stocked. When you and your team are on top of these tasks with a clear purpose you will get many positive comments.

Just as a side note, what I see often in toilet facilities are checklists. This is to show that they are checked for all the reasons that have been mentioned. It is concerning when you can see the checklist signed off at the time you have visited the loo, yet it looks and feels awful. This is called a 'tick box exercise'—literally!

CONSIDER any of the loos in your business:
- Have you considered the feel of the toilet tissue?
- Is the loo experience aligned to the experience you and your customers want, need and expect?
- Are your hand drying facilities aligned to your overall aim?

In a luxury establishment, paper hand drying facilities are not appropriate for a luxurious experience. Fresh, fluffy individual towels, however (in my opinion), are. The most important thing is that drying facilities are plentiful and clean and the experience your customers have is a positive one.

Super wet surfaces are also often the case at pubs and bars, the bar frequently swimming in beer or other liquids. It's important to consider what this is like for your customers. In many cases, they have dressed up for a great night out, made an effort to look and feel good. Yet they get covered in liquid as soon as they stand close to the busy and sometimes overcrowded bar.

Be clear about what you want your customers to experience.

In order to get your customers feeling good about what they touch whilst in your business, it needs to feel clean, smooth and dry. Surely you are striving to build their confidence in your product or service. To take this to being exceptional, they would feel materials aligned to what you're striving to achieve, whether this is luxury or rustic.

Now to move on to the atmospheric feel to your business.

The atmosphere

Customers can immediately pick up on the atmosphere in a business—the 'vibe'. This can attract or detract, depending on your personal preference. It is generated by the behaviours of the people within the business, whether these are the customers or colleagues.

We've all walked along the street and been attracted to enter a bar, restaurant or café because of the perceived atmosphere—it's busy and the people seem to be having a great time.

On the other hand, you have probably almost run out of some places as there's a feeling of animosity, whether this is in a busy or quiet place. I've stepped into coffee shops and even asked the staff if everything is alright as I can sense a negative feeling in the air. I've mentioned to the staff member that they don't seem too happy and they've explained that their boss or colleague has upset them in some way. This links with 'hear'—what your team is sharing with your customers. The way your team is treated will impact on their spirit. I like people to be honest; if they're unhappy, it can be difficult to hide or put on the 'service show'.

Beware, as I'm sure you will know, that there are people who are naturally mood vacuums (mood hoovers!); they zap any positive vibes and regurgitate this energy to impose negativity on others. This can, if persistent, have a gloomy impact on other people's moods. Whilst there are other people who are radiators, who ooze positive energy. Likewise, this can influence other people positively and switch a perceived grey day into sunshine and blue skies. Not everyone is emotionally in tune with atmospheric situations, but many are.

The behavioural hustle and bustle of people within your business is important. Are people happy, calm and complementing the overall purpose, design and aspirations for your business?

CASE STUDY

There's nothing quite like the atmosphere in a sporting stadium when the team you are supporting are winning throughout the game and eventually win. I once had the opportunity to watch Manchester United when they won the league, which led to other wins for that year. It was amazing! The people behind the bar were in good spirits and making small talk about the game. Everyone close to where we were standing were making positive comments about the players and the game's progress. The players did their thing, played well, were focused and delivering to the supporters' expectations. When the final whistle was blown, the whole stadium erupted with cheers. You had to be there to feel this electric atmosphere. There's no way you could have replicated it. I'll never forget it. It was awesome!

On reflection from this, consider:
- Where have you been where the atmosphere has been electric?
- What made it so special?

Here are a few of my thoughts:
- The ongoing performance of this team created the excitement amongst their customers...the supporters.
- All the staff, including the players, showed their commitment to the sport and what their customers buy into.
- There wasn't one person who wasn't happy to be there; they also created the excitement in anticipation for a win.
- Teams who perform well gain loyal followers.
- The culture that has been created over time ensures that their customers behave appropriately to make the experience safe and enjoyable.

Thinking about your business:
- Do you and your team create an atmosphere that supports the purpose of your business?
- Do you and your team know what needs to be done to create loyal customers?
- Do you and your team create a feel and atmosphere that leads your customers to feel safe and secure within your business?
- Do you and your team feel focused to ensure that they win? Do you and your team get that winning vibe that creates energy and passion to want to win again?

It is worth noting that should your customers be causing any negative vibes, what action is taken to ensure the atmosphere remains welcoming. Are your team trained and do they know how to handle such situations? Where will they gain support? Customers who create these bad vibes are likely to impact on other customers. The ones you want to keep. Balancing this is tricky, however it's important that appropriate behaviours are expected from everyone.

Behaviour plays a huge part in how others feel.

Give this the attention that it deserves to ensure your customers feel only positivity as a result of their experience with you, your colleagues and your business.

Temperature

Another aspect to consider is whether there are any drafts your customers may notice and be sensitive to. If you want your customers to be comfortable whilst in your business, you will give this some attention. A guy I once met asked me, 'What's the difference between a draft and fresh air?' The response he gave was, 'Fresh air is when you open the window. A draft is when someone else opens the window.' Be mindful of who you're trying to please.

The temperature of your premises needs to meet your customer requirements. An ice-rink clearly needs to be cold; it doesn't take long to warm up once on the rink! However, the spectators will freeze if they sit still for long enough. When customers visit a sauna, it needs to be hot. If the sauna is not to the correct high temperature, it doesn't have the desired effect.

Of course, these are extremes and there are many temperatures in between that would be suitable for your business. However, should it be the same temperature throughout? Should some rooms be warmer than others, e.g. in a pub, on a cold winter's night with an open fire, creating a warm and cosy atmosphere to encourage customers to stay and drink for longer. Or a shopping centre that is cool on a hot sunny day, to encourage them to spend more time shopping, keeping cool and making it a pleasant and enjoyable experience. In a hotel, it would feel uncomfortable if the whole building was warm and cosy, it may feel stuffy. Ideally the corridors would be cooler than the bar. The bedrooms not too hot yet not freezing, to be slightly cooler than the bar or lounge area.

Whilst we're talking about fresh air, it doesn't take long for a closed space to feel humid and uncomfortable.

Air circulation is important to ensure the customers are feeling fresh, awake and maintain their energy levels.

Stale air is not good for anybody's well-being. Damp in the air is also bad for everyone's health. If this is the case for your business, consider what might need altering.

Once again, it is important to know and understand the wants, needs and expectations of your customers. It is only then that you can provide the atmosphere that is suitable for them and makes them want to return.

Notes

FEEL EXCEPTIONAL CHECKLIST PART ONE

Take a walk around your business. Notice what you feel within the air, atmosphere, floor and surfaces. Consider the following questions and make a list of the things that you do well.

Feel exceptional service standards:

Are all areas where your customers sit or stand free from drafts?	Y ☐	N ☐
Do your customers feel clean, polished surfaces?	Y ☐	N ☐
Do your customers feel clean, polished surfaces underfoot?	Y ☐	N ☐
Do your customers feel clean and freshly vacuumed flooring?	Y ☐	N ☐
Do your customers feel quality products aligned to your business style?	Y ☐	Y ☐
Do your customers feel dry (where required—this wouldn't work in a swimming pool or spa!) surfaces throughout your business?	Y ☐	N ☐
Do you feel positive vibes coming from your colleagues? Do they seem calm, confident and happy in their role?	Y ☐	N ☐
Do you feel positive vibes when your colleagues interact with each other?	Y ☐	N ☐
Do you feel positive vibes coming from your customers? If not, what action needs to be taken? Do your team know what to do about this kind of situation?	Y ☐	N ☐
Do your customers feel the temperature is at the right level for their comfort?	Y ☐	N ☐
Do your customers feel the atmosphere is clean and fresh? Not humid, damp or stale.	Y ☐	N ☐

Which of these do you already do consistently?

Celebrate what you notice you and your team well. Encourage them to maintain this consistently. Share what you have noticed with your team, so they are likely to continue to create that feel-good factor and high standards.

Select the one service standards you want to upgrade or improve within your business and note it here:

Select one point for now, as we're about to consider the second part of feel from the 'emotional' perspective.

#	SERVICE STANDARDS CHECKLIST	YES/NO
1	**Does the entrance have an attractive curb appeal?** *(See)*	No
	What did you observe/notice? Weeds around the edge of the building and in the gutter in front of our premises. The windows were smeared and there were weeds next to the business signage.	
2	**Are all colleagues looking clean, smart and well presented?** *(See)*	Yes
	What did you observe/notice? Jane and Richard in clean company uniform. Ironed shirts and no stains.	
3	**Do your customers hear positive background music and noise? i.e. no slamming doors, maintenance or clattering from the team?** *(Hear)*	No
	What did you observe/notice? The door going into the admin office bangs each time it closes.	
4	**Are all the team engaging with customers using positive language?** *(Hear)*	Yes
	What did you observe/notice? Sandy greeted the customer with 'Mr Palmer, how are you today?'	
5	**Do your premises smell fresh and aired?** *(Smell)*	Yes
	What did you observe/notice? No unpleasant odours. Could potentially feel more aired.	

SERVICE STANDARDS CHECKLIST	YES/NO
6 **Do all your toilet facilities smell fresh and aired?** *(Smell)* **What did you observe/notice?** A strong smell of chemicals in the loos.	No
7 **Are all hot foods & drinks service on hot/warm crockery?** *(Taste)* **What did you observe/notice?** All plates serving hot food felt warm. Napkins available for customers to hold their plates.	Yes
8 **Are all cold foods and drinks served in cold glassware or crockery?** *(Taste)* **What did you observe/notice?** A strong smell of chemicals in the loos.	No
9 **Do all surfaces feel clean, fresh & polished? Not sticky, slippery, slimy, dusty or dirty.** *(Feel)* **What did you observe/notice?** The coffee table in the lobby had a stain on it and was sticky.	No

Take into account the customers' perspective of what they feel in the air, on surfaces, flooring and in the loo. It is important that these details are noticed by everyone in your business.

Take a close look at your notes from Chapter 1. Is the environment best suited to meet your customers' expectations? What ambience would you like to create to reassure your customers? Remember, how your team behave will play a big part in this.

As mentioned, the physical 'feel' is just part of the story. Let's take a closer look at the emotional connections your customers 'feel'.

Notes

WHAT WE WANT OUR CUSTOMERS TO FEEL... EMOTIONALLY CONNECTED

L et us now consider the emotional 'feel'. How do you want your customers to feel about your business? This is how all the senses are brought together and is how you will build your customer loyalty, creating an environment where they are emotionally connected to you, your team and business.

Your customer leaves thinking that their visit was exceptional, with the feeling that they want to return time and time again. This is about making the customer feel special, that they are considered and that you have recognised their special occasions, or their uniqueness that may require a spot of additional attention.

This doesn't need to cost, simply be considered. In today's day and age, social media is king. People are much more likely to share positive experiences of a creative folded towel, or a note wishing them a good day or happy birthday.

Everyone—even those who are less in touch with their emotions—will FEEL a certain way (and come to a conclusion) about your business based on what they see, hear, taste, smell and touch.

Creating an experience which results in a positive emotion connects your customers to your business.

The flipside is that an experience could give them a negative feeling—not ideal! If this is the case, it can have the opposite effect of turning them off your establishment for life. It's possibly the most important aspect of all and is the outcome of all the five senses.

When you have the five senses in place—the basics, as I call it—this emotional feel is the icing on the cake. There are some places I have visited where the emotional connection is there, however the basics are not in place. This is the case in a local coffee shop; the team is lovely, super friendly. They have good fun with the regulars, yet the front doors are covered in fingerprints, the toilets are smelly, the table tops are often sticky and full of crumbs. The emotional connection does result in an enjoyable experience, but it would be even better if the five senses were also attended to.

Some people are good at doing this, it's second nature for them. Yet there are far more people who don't have a clue, or at least don't even try to make a personal connection with other people.

CONSIDER:

- Do you and all members in your team acknowledge all customers as they appear or enter your business or the employee's area of work?
- Do you and all members in your team engage with all customers in a positive manner?
- Do you and all members in your team listen carefully to your customers?
- Do you and all members in your team seem pleased to interact with your customers?
- Do you believe that all your customers leave your business feeling valued and considered?

People make the difference

As you know, I have been fortunate to work in and therefore visit many fabulous five-star hotels. In many, the entrances are grand. What you see are beautiful furnishings and carpets, you hear unobtrusive music, people talking discreetly, the smells are warm and calming, the cushions and coffee tables feel smooth and luxurious. Yet so often, the staff don't give an instant and genuine welcome with eye contact. A welcome that is heartfelt is what makes a positive difference. This needs to happen for all customers at all times. It is not easy, unless all your team understand what good or great service looks and feels like. There is the added challenge of us all being different, with some members of staff taking to it better than others. This can leave your customers with inconsistent experiences. However, with good training and confidence building, it is possible to ensure that every member of your team understands.

One of the hotels I managed was in desperate need of investment. However, it was clean and tidy. In other words, we did our best to make the most of the premises and furnishings that we had. As a result, the focus was on us, the staff. The whole mantra was that customers would come to the hotel to see us, not the hotel! We oozed hospitality and took good care of all our customers. It worked. The hotel was the most efficient in the company at converting revenue into profit. This led to confidence and investment in the property and an overdue upgrade. Exceptional service, in all circumstances, works.

On the next page is a story that a colleague shared with me. As you read, consider the customer's feelings throughout. You might have experienced something similar yourself.

Notes

CASE STUDY

My colleague was expecting her first child, obviously a new experience for her. She was given the choice of a midwife or to see the GP (doctor), and decided to go to the GP. Having booked online, she received no confirmation. This was her first appointment to learn about what to expect during her pregnancy, what to look out for and how to ensure she and the baby kept well and monitored. A friend had told her that a urine test would be suggested at this stage of her pregnancy. During her appointment, she asked the GP about this, and the GP replied that this was to be done at a later stage. She left after 10 minutes, no wiser about what to expect. Her impression was that the doctor was flippant, offering no clarity about the next steps. At a time of excitement, joy mixed with uncertainty, and feeling a little anxious about the unknown and wanting to know how to ensure the well-being of her baby and herself, she left her doctor even more anxious than when she went in. The outcome is that she went to find an alternative GP.

On reflection from this, consider:
- Is the doctor thinking from the patient's perspective?
- If the doctor gave some consideration to how this patient might be feeling, having her first child, what information, clarity and reassurance might she need?
- How could the doctor have shown more care with this patient?

Before thinking about your business, here are a few of my thoughts:
- This doctor 'processed' my colleague. I can imagine that they see expectant mothers all the time and couldn't be bothered to consider her feelings at all.
- Showing that you care about your customers is important. When considering people's lives, this is even more critical.
- Had they responded with more empathy and compassion connected to the urine test and explained the next steps, it would have been more likely that she'd leave reassured and happy. This may have led to her staying with that practice.
- When you genuinely care, other people can tell. It shows. I get the impression that this doctor didn't really care. I'm sure they have great technical ability as a qualified doctor, however they were not emotionally connected to the needs of their patient.

Thinking about your business:
- Can you relate any parallels from this story to what might be happening in your business? Capture your thoughts about what you'd like your customers to be feeling after visiting you.

CASE STUDY

An example of great service is at my local petrol station. It makes me smile and, out of choice, I would always go there for fuel. What makes it memorable and special is that the cashiers look at you as you approach to pay. They ask 'How are you today?' first, then which pump you've used, or if you're the only car on the forecourt, they check the pump number with you. As they process the payment, the conversation continues. It's lovely and friendly. However, I notice that they gauge whether their customers want this chat or not. As I stand in the queue, they approach each customer in the same way. If the customer is abrupt to them and direct, they don't tend to pursue a conversation. The payment transaction doesn't take any longer than at other petrol stations who just tell you how much you owe (Sometimes not even that—I've been in petrol stations where the service provider is on the phone and just points at the amount on the till and says nothing at all. I've just spent a fair amount of money and they've not even said 'thank you'. I don't go back. It's rude). The team at my favourite petrol station always say 'thank you' and wish you a good day, which sounds sincere. They don't use the same farewell expression to everyone; it's the one that is appropriate to the customer. They once asked me about my plans for the weekend. I said that I was going to the races. On this occasion, the farewell they used was 'I hope those horses do well for you.' Gorgeous.

On reflection from this, consider:
- What stands out to you from this example?

Before thinking about your business, here are a few of my thoughts:
- The team in the petrol station show a genuine interest in their customers.
- They flex their approach to the needs of each individual customer.
- They are consistent in their desire to engage with their customers. Well, at least in my experience this is the case.

Thinking about your business:
- What positive points can you take from this example that you might want to include in your checklists, perhaps now or in the future?

Good and not-so-good experiences are easily shared on social media. It's so easy to tell others, then within seconds...boom, many people know.

It would be amazing if customers felt appreciated as one of the most valued elements of your business.

After all, without your customers, your business is NOTHING.

Being genuine and real is SO important. My last few visits to the United States have been nothing but disappointing. I visited Florida a number of years ago and thought the whole experience was 'WOW'. Although at times I would question how genuine the service was. People have been known to rave about service in the US. I'm not so sure. Here are just a few examples to put this into context.

A recent experience back in Florida at a well-known theme park where the spirit seemed flat and not at all what I remembered from my previous visit. There seemed to be an air of 'we can't be bothered'. What was even more concerning was that the prices were very high. Now you pay for each day of parking, which isn't cheap. We also had the privilege of queues like I've never experienced before. Queues that are predicted to be up to 5 hours long (yep, 5 hours) for just one ride that might last 3 minutes. It left me feeling ripped off and believing that this company has become greedy. The parks can't cope with the number of visitors they have.

One experience in particular sticks in my mind.

CASE STUDY

Whilst we were there, we visited a family restaurant that I used to enjoy visiting over 20 years ago. It was the biggest disappointment. The product was tired, with no investment. It seemed much worse than I remembered it. The food and the service were terrible. We had to wait over 30 minutes for a table, and when we did get a table the service was very slow. We had to ask to place our food order and chase the order, which didn't come out together. The toilets were dirty and left me wondering what state the kitchen would be in. I felt that I had let my family down. Actually, one family member was ill afterwards, just as we left to fly home, and we believe it was as a result of the breakfast we had in this restaurant. I was also confused. I couldn't understand why there were so many people waiting to dine there when it was awful.

On reflection from this, consider:
- What would have been the biggest issue for you in this situation?
- Are you able to relate to this situation in any way as a customer?
- Have you had a continual great experience with a product or service then been disappointed or let down?

Before thinking about your business, here are a few of my thoughts:
- Maybe many of their customers are 'one time' visitors to Florida, so it doesn't matter?
- The customers who were waiting to experience this restaurant will not be back.
- The process of ensuring the five senses of the customers was not considered at all.
- The kitchen was probably even more dirty than the toilets, the team didn't care, the food tasted awful or average, the service was not prioritised.
- I will never go back, although it's not likely we shall visit Florida again very soon. However, if I hear of any family or friends going, I shall highly recommend that they avoid this family diner chain.
- There was no apology offered for anything. We were processed through a system.
- If they had considered the five senses along with efficient ways of working and had taken a frequent walk in their customers' shoes, what huge improvements could have been made? How many more loyal customers would this generate? How many people who visit once in a lifetime would recommend that restaurant to friends and family when they visit? I think there are so many missed opportunities. I wished they cared or at least seemed to care.

Thinking about your business:
- How do you engage with customers who may be waiting to place orders or use your services?
- How do you and your team behave when you notice that your customers may have experienced delays?
- Are you and your team behaving in a way that is likely to give your customers the impression that you care about them?

You might have the impression that I have something against the United States of America; however, I'd like to reassure you that I don't. The reason for me sharing these examples is as a result of me noticing that in the past, generally speaking, I've heard others say (and thought myself) that this was one place where they seemed to get service right. I know there are many organisations who do, which leaves me being loyal to these brands. It also shows that the way customers, patients, students, clients, guests and passengers are treated by the people within your organisation make lasting impressions, memories that potentially will last forever. One bad experience encountered by a number of people might leave your business at a point of no return as a result of damage that has been done.

If you want to build a reputation for being great to exceptional, one thing is true:

> *There is no room for complacency when it comes to looking after your customers.*

This sense of feeling and being emotionally connected is so problematic due the complexity of each and every person that you interact with who may want to buy from you. Here's an example where you might think I was being awkward. (Actually, you might think this about all the examples in this book!) It's another US example. Sorry.

During a trip to New York, we jumped in a cab from the airport to the hotel. The cab driver was on and off the brakes, jerking the car all the way. I felt sick. When we arrived, we paid him the fare quoted. He stood waiting for his tip. We responded with 'no', as it was an awful journey and we had no low change to give, only high dollar notes (we had just arrived). This was an awful first impression for New York. Surely he knew that people travelling from the airport often have little spare change, or does he expect a tip of one of those high dollar notes? Probably the latter! The point for me is the driver expected a tip, even when the experience literally left me feeling sick. I realise the tipping culture is very different in the US compared with the UK; however, the lasting feeling was poor and of course has left me telling everyone about the experience. (I could write a book about a tipping culture too and how it impacts on service!)

Know your stuff

From what we experience as customers, we make our judgment by gathering data through our senses and make decisions on whether to return or not.

This data leads to whether or not our customers feel confident in our businesses. Customers want to feel you know what you're doing. It's through how they see you behave, what is said and how it is said that leads to customers feeling assured that they are in good hands. This supports what was outlined in the 'hear' chapter.

Be genuine, real and considered

The service provided needs to be genuine and give the feeling that you and your team feel confident and proud to do what you do. If you're not, then something needs to change; it has to be upgraded and reviewed.

CONSIDER:

- Are you confident that your customers are likely to recommend you to others?
- Are you confident that your service delivery is consistent?
- How often do you assess your customers' experience aligned to the standards that you set?

The magic is all about assessing what is needed and considering the wants and needs of each individual customer, then flexing to meet their needs. We are human beings not robots, so we cannot treat everyone the same. What makes us different are our feelings and emotions.

If you can provide an emotional connection each and every time your customers interact with your business, it is set for success.

As your customers notice your body language, tone of voice and the words that you use, you can do the same to them. From this information, you can respond appropriately. The intention of looking after the customer remains the same; how you do it makes the difference. You might alter your facial expression from being happy and bouncy to calm and considered when you notice the customer looking serious or stern. It's almost like mirroring the customer. Many people do this naturally; however, there are so many who don't.

Overall, the skill is to ensure you consider each customer as though they are the first customer you have interacted with that day.

Once you are confident that you have considered each of the five senses and that what your customers experience every time is aligned with their personal taste, you can move on to taking your business to the next phase.

Being clear about how you want your customers to feel is one big step forward to being exceptional. This is why the checklists are so useful in taking doable steps towards your ideal. What you select on your checklists will depend on where you are currently and where you want your business to be.

When we as customers are given personal attention,
when we are acknowledged and given some consideration,
we are left feeling warm and valued.

It's so simple, I really don't know why it's not done all of the time. Your business will flourish and grow, with an abundance of loyal customers who are confident to recommend you, your product and service with passion and reassurance. The best kind of marketing any business could ask for.

Notes

FEEL EXCEPTIONAL CHECKLIST PART TWO

Take a look at how you and your team behave around your customers (and maybe each other), as you walk around your business. Consider these questions and make a list of the positive things you notice.

Feel exceptional service standards:

Do you and your team greet and acknowledge your customer as soon as they arrive into your business or premises?	Y ☐	N ☐
Do you and your team greet and acknowledge your customers as they move around your business or premises?	Y ☐	N ☐
Do you and your team seem to genuinely want to look after your customers?	Y ☐	N ☐
Do you and your team seem to genuinely care about your customers?	Y ☐	N ☐
Do you and your team ask if they can assist further at appropriate times for your customer?	Y ☐	Y ☐
Do you and your team make eye contact with your customers?	Y ☐	N ☐
Do you and your team display open and welcoming body language that gives the customer the impression that you care?	Y ☐	N ☐
Do you and your team communicate with your customers in a caring tone of voice?	Y ☐	N ☐
Do you and your team communicate calmly and with confidence with your customers?	Y ☐	N ☐
Do you and your team consider ways of making a customers' experience memorable? Such as a note of thanks to them, a note wishing them a happy birthday or anniversary, finding something out about them and offering assistance with this.	Y ☐	N ☐
Do you and your team ask genuinely how your customer's experience was? With the intention of learning from that customer experience and gaining information to potentially improve for the future.	Y ☐	N ☐
Do you and your team offer a genuine 'farewell' to your customers? With a message along the lines of 'We look forward to seeing you again'.	Y ☐	N ☐

Which of these do you already do consistently?

Celebrate what you notice you and your team do well. Encourage them to maintain this consistently. Share what you have noticed with your team, so they are likely to continue to create that feel-good factor and perform well.

Select the one service standards you want to upgrade or improve within your business and note it here:

Select one point to complete your initial observation sheet. Keep your *Service Standards Checklists* to 10 points to make it doable for you and your team. This will also make it easier for the whole team to master as a starting point, creating a feel-good factor for you and your team within your business.

SERVICE STANDARDS CHECKLIST		YES/ NO
1	**Does the entrance have an attractive curb appeal?** *(See)*	No
	What did you observe/notice? Weeds around the edge of the building and in the gutter in front of our premises. The windows were smeared and there were weeds next to the business signage.	
2	**Are all colleagues looking clean, smart and well presented?** *(See)*	Yes
	What did you observe/notice? Jane and Richard in clean company uniform. Ironed shirts and no stains.	
3	**Do your customers hear positive background music and noise? i.e. no slamming doors, maintenance or clattering from the team?** *(Hear)*	No
	What did you observe/notice? The door going into the admin office bangs each time it closes.	

SERVICE STANDARDS CHECKLIST		YES/ NO
4	**Are all the team engaging with customers using positive language?** *(Hear)*	Yes
	What did you observe/notice? Sandy greeted the customer with 'Mr Palmer, how are you today?'	
5	**Do your premises smell fresh and aired?** *(Smell)*	Yes
	What did you observe/notice? No unpleasant odours. Could potentially feel more aired.	
6	**Do all your toilet facilities smell fresh and aired?** *(Smell)*	No
	What did you observe/notice? A strong smell of chemicals in the loos.	
7	**Are all hot foods & drinks service on hot/warm crockery?** *(Taste)*	Yes
	What did you observe/notice? All plates serving hot food felt warm. Napkins available for customers to hold their plates.	
8	**Are all cold foods and drinks served in cold glassware or crockery?** *(Taste)*	No
	What did you observe/notice? A strong smell of chemicals in the loos.	
9	**Do all surfaces feel clean, fresh & polished? Not sticky, slippery, slimy, dusty or dirty.** *(Feel)*	No
	What did you observe/notice? The coffee table in the lobby had a stain on it and was sticky.	
10	**Do all team members instantly and genuinely welcome all of your customers?** *(Feel)*	No
	What did you observe/notice? 2 did, 1 did after a few seconds, 1 didn't and was more interested in looking at the computer.	
Total: **Comments/What have you learned?**		4/10 =40%

Now you have a completed *Service Standards Checklist*, make a start on using it. If you are a leading a team of people, share with them your aspirations of upgrading the customer experience. Encourage them to assess themselves. Make this part of your daily routine, just like you do with your sale takings. Assess how you are doing, learn from what you do well and what might be overlooked until you master these initial 10 points. There is more about implementing the *10-Service Standards Checklists* in Chapter 10 — 'Be exceptional'.

Ensure that you appreciate the value your team brings to the service that is provided in your business. When they are feeling good about the role they play it is noticed by everyone else, the customer especially.

When your customers receive a consistent good service from your team, your business is on the right lines to flourish and grow.

Consistency drives confidence, confidence drives loyalty.

In the next chapter, the focus will shift from creating the foundational sensory standards for all customers to considering the needs of each individual customer, one person at a time. We will talk about the customer feeling considered and valued, an important part of taking that step to being exceptional.

Notes

STAGE 2.
ONE CUSTOMER

Behaving in a way that emotionally
connects with 'one customer'
at one time.

6 STEPS TO
EXCEPTIONAL
SERVICE

U p to now you have considered the five senses and prioritised two service standards from each of the five that you'd like to see you and your team deliver. These are the basic standards that are to be shared with your team so they can make a start in making these happen. Remember to celebrate team successes so that you and they feel confident in knowing what good looks and feels like.

Having reflected on your progress so far in providing an excellent service to your customers, now it is time to move on to providing an exceptional service for each individual customer. This means:

placing the 'one' customer at the centre of everything you and your team do.

It is time to create an exceptional emotional connection with your customer.

CONSIDER:

- Have you ensured that the basic and sensory needs of all you customers are in place, as we've explored so far? If so, now is the time to consider what else you need to know and learn about your customers.
- What are the cultural wants and needs of the customers you want to attract to your business—maybe you can work this out from how they live? For example, some cultures expect things to be delivered 'now', others '10-minutes ago', some are laid back and expect things 'eventually, when you're ready'.
- What are the cultural expectations of the organisations you work with? For example, is Corporate and Social Responsibility (CSR) valued by them? What can you do so you are considerate of these values?
- How do you gather information about what your customers expect, want and need? What will you do to gain this information?

This is often called 'World Class Service'. I hear this expression used frequently, yet I'm not sure it is fully understood. Having worked in places that really do offer 'World-Class Service', I know that they can flex their service or product to meet the needs of their customers. World-Class Service is the mindset of being curious in how you can respond to your customers' needs.

Instead of processing all customers in the same way, in a way that suits the service provider or business owner, it's about dealing with each individual customer and their wants and needs with a mindset of knowing you will achieve it.

Here's an example of the service delivery changing in accordance with the cultural needs of the customer.

Notes

CASE STUDY

As I'm sure you're aware, in exclusive and informal hotel restaurants, evening dining would be pre-prepared for service. Anticipating the guests who are booked to arrive when the restaurant opens from 7pm, the restaurant would be immaculate, and tables all set by 5pm. The team would follow the usual service expected in a formal restaurant: three course meals, where you choose from a menu, select what you'd like, then order. The starter would be served first, then main course, followed by dessert then coffee, with liqueurs also offered. A dining experience from start to finish would generally take about 90 minutes.

At a 'World-Class Service' hotel in London where international customers (guests) would stay frequently, the restaurant team would often receive a call at 6pm from a Middle Eastern guest requesting a table for 20 people within the next 20 minutes. No matter who or what other table reservations were already booked in, the table would be created. The table would be set less formally than normal, only one set of knives and forks, rather than side-plate, starter cutlery, etc. The guests would arrive and the food (which had been outlined when making the bedroom reservation, not knowing when they might be dining) would be placed in the centre of the table within a minute of them arriving. They would help themselves to the food they wanted, eat, eat and eat then leave. Within 25 minutes of them arriving they would have left. The team would then rearrange the restaurant ready for their first guests to arrive.

On reflection from this, consider:
- What mindset do these colleagues have?
- What preparation needed to be considered?
- What impact do you believe this type of business would have on the overall results for that restaurant?

Before thinking about your business, here are a few of my thoughts:
- Clients from the Middle East were of huge value to the hotel and restaurant.
- The teams from all departments made it their business to gather as much information as possible about the guests' needs and expectations ahead of their stay or visit. They shared this information with appropriate teams within the hotel so their expectations were met, if not even exceeded.
- The restaurant team worked together to change things around as a matter of urgency for the Middle Eastern guests and to then switch back ready for all the guests already booked in. It was an all-round win.
- The culture within this restaurant and hotel was 'the first response to our guest's needs will never be no.'
- Sometimes what customers want is not always doable; however, it's how you respond that will make you exceptional. Explore what you can do; consider offering

alternative solutions. Maybe even recommend a supplier who you believe would be able to assist if you cannot accommodate their demands. Customers will remember your helpful approach.

Thinking about your business:

- What demands have you noticed that your customers put on you?
- Some customers have expectations that seem impossible; how can you make it possible? This is what will make your business stand out from the rest.
- When will you ask your customers what exactly they want and need, so you can respond in the best way to meet these expectations?

The reason why this was successful was because the hotel applied the 6 steps to creating an emotional connection with their guests, with the aim of creating a reputation that leaves the customers emotionally attached. It is important to ensure these are applied consistently throughout the whole experience: at the beginning, middle and end.

The six steps to be exceptional are as follows:

1. Be there
2. Watch for the signals
3. Ask questions
4. Listen
5. Respond
6. Make it memorable

When you are being fully present for your customers, you have a mindset of knowing what is important to the customer and how you can make it happen.

Keeping this focus will ensure your greatest asset is always considered. Have the aim of generating exceptional results, including returning business and gaining confident recommendations from your loyal customers, both of which create revenue generation. Your team makes the difference. Refer to p.96 where I talk about my experience working in the hotel that was in desperate need of refurbishment. It was the team who generated the additional sales. Without sales, we have nothing...no business...nothing.

Whilst examining each step in turn, you may find it useful to make notes as you read on to gather what this might mean for your business. This will then assist you in creating the next level of *Service Standards Checklist*, which will lead you to being exceptional. The timing of when you do this all depends on where your service levels are at currently. Please remember the purpose of this book is for you to be honest with yourself and ensure 'the basics' of the other senses are in place first. If you don't, it is like building a house with no foundation.

Let's start at the obvious place, step 1.

Be there

I guess this speaks for itself. However, I don't often notice or sense this as a customer. It is not always easy as many businesses have a small number of staff per customer, but there are ways to address this without going overboard.

A smile and a nod of the head to greet a customer goes a long way to them feeling valued.

This is very simple; in order to look after your customers, you need to 'be there', or at least someone in your team needs to be present. It doesn't matter how wonderful the environment may be, without a person present to create a welcome or acknowledgement that you are available to assist your customer, there is no experience.

Picture this: a gorgeous ornate reception, beautifully decorated with luxurious fixtures and fittings, with no one present? It gives the impression of a ghost town, no life. This is what a business feels like when there is no one 'being there'.

People are the key to bringing life to your business.

I realise that we all have our diverse perspectives on how we like to experience 'be there', and this is why it is important that you create what your customers want. Here are some examples from my perspective, the only perspective I can give, of course!

The first example is, for me, where 'being there' is inappropriate or too much. I've walked into shoe shops, and as soon as I have entered through the door the sales assistant has said, 'Good morning, what are you looking for today?' This, for me, is pressure. Shoe shopping is something I do by seeing what's available and then I am potentially inspired, before deciding if they match what I might want or need.

I realise other people may know exactly what they want and be able to state this. In this circumstance the customer would be taken to the area aligned to their needs. Which is great. My only concern with this is that they miss the opportunity to notice any other shoes during their search and therefore are not tempted to buy something else.

What is great about this example is the customer is acknowledged, which is SO much better than being ignored, or not being noticed at all.

Being there for your customers is the most important of tasks, ahead of others such as stocking the shelves, vacuuming the floor, briefing the team, chatting about last night with colleagues, etc. Yet, in most places I go it seems that completing tasks take the priority. What goes through my head is 'Will that task generate more revenue for your business?' Your customers' perception or experience will. Ignoring them generates a perception that this task is more important than them. It's simple:

Customer FIRST, task second.

My mantra is:

Make it easy for your customer to spend money.

There is also another financial implication to 'Be there'. When you acknowledge customers over completing tasks, you are saying to the customer 'I've noticed you'. This will deter shoplifters from helping themselves to your stock, as they may do if they notice you concentrating on the task. I challenge anyone to switch their approach to be customer first and see what happens. I often walk into retail outlets and no one acknowledges me, where I walk past so many people who don't even know that someone has walked through their department or store. This is SO worrying. The purpose of your business is to embrace customers as they are your lifeline. Organisations spend a fortune on marketing, selling, and promoting their business to entice customers to buy, yet when the customer turns up they are ignored. It blows my mind!

This is not difficult or complicated. It's simply acknowledging people, whether this is eye contact, a nod of the head, a greeting of 'hi' if in an informal service environment or choose the appropriate acknowledgement to the time of day—'Good morning', 'Good afternoon' or 'Good evening'—in a formal establishment. It needs to be visible throughout the experience to complement the style and culture of your business and ideal customer. The most important thing is that everyone in the business looks up when a customer enters and uses their body language to say, 'I see you and I'm here to assist if and when you're ready.'

You often see staff with what seems like tunnel vision, as though they are wearing blinkers. They're on a mission to get from one side of the business to the other and don't want to be noticed or notice others. Please note, this is observed by customers—they can see you and they recognise this body language, as we examined in the 'See' chapter. The message is loud and clear: 'I don't want to be bothered by you, don't talk to me.' When I have been a customer who needed a helping hand to spend some money within a business, I have stopped people like this. It's quite entertaining. They act all surprised as though they didn't expect to meet a customer on the shop floor. They then fob you off with, 'it's out of stock' or 'it's on the far side of the store.' Wouldn't it be amazing if this situation could be flipped to, 'Hi, how can I help you? Let me go and check.' Then they go out of their way to ensure you get exactly what you want, even if this means ordering one for you. It's so easy; make sure they spend money with you and not your competition.

Colleagues chatting to each other in front of the customer was mentioned in the 'Hear' chapter; this is another example of not being there for the customer. Any conversation should be secondary to acknowledging the customer. It's not difficult to make this a priority: eye contact, a smile and a nod of the head is all it takes. I've even seen leaders briefing their team as the customer waits to be looked after. This tells me the leader has lost the plot. I'm sure they are all wrapped up in needing to generate important reports for their big bosses about the performance of their store or department. They'll have to justify why sales are up or down, etc. However, it's ironic that they won't have any reports to generate if they continue to treat their customers in this way. Customers will simply visit your competitors and take their business there. As soon as any leader takes priority over the customer, the message is lost. Everything anyone in a business does should be putting the customer FIRST. Without them you will have no business to report on.

Whilst we're on the subject of conversations, the phone is an important example of 'be there'. When a customer is phoning your business, they want to be answered. If not, it gives the impression that you are not being there for them. Over the many years of working with customers, there is debate over whether you are to look after the person in front of you or the ringing phone first. Say 'Would you excuse me for a moment whilst I get this call?' Gain the permission of the person in front of you. If they say 'no', then carry on with them. Let us come back to this in the next step, 'watch the signals'. Ideally, a phone would be answered in person within three rings for the customer to feel that you are there for them.

The first acknowledgement is so important. You will notice that exclusive businesses appoint a doorman whose sole purpose is to acknowledge EVERYONE who enters the business, and it sets the tone for the whole experience. A warm, genuine welcome with the door opened for you is polite and considered. Where a doorman is not appointed, anyone in your team in any type of business can create this welcome when they are watching what is happening and looking out for the arrival of the next customer.

Here's an example to put this into context. I had been working with a construction company who have been hugely successful. They've recently invested in their premises and workshops. They are impressive, a real showcase of the work they do. They have customers visit their premises. However, this is not like a shop, so visitors come every once in a while. Hence, they have a buzzer on the door, which the admin staff respond to. There have been times when I've stood at the door about to press the buzzer and a member of staff walks straight past the door. This could be because they genuinely didn't see me. If this is the case, in order to adopt an 'exceptional' experience, the team would be looking out for potential visitors as they move around the building. Or secondly, it could be that they couldn't be bothered and chose to ignore someone at the door. Either way, in this case the behaviour of the team doesn't complement the stunning premises. I could potentially leave with a niggle in my mind that although they clearly do a great job, what would they be like to work with when the team seem to have an arrogant, can't-be-bothered attitude.

Overall, the first step to being exceptional is that you need to 'be there' for all of your customers, giving the first impression that 'we're here for you and we've noticed you, and you are THE most important in our world right now.' This needs to be the case throughout the whole experience. There should not be a time when the customer feels that they have been abandoned. Being there will lead to their loyalty and will build your reputation as the obvious business to recommend to others. As I've said before, this is the best kind of marketing any business could possibly ask for.

CONSIDER:

- What level of attention do you want your customer to have as they arrive into your business? Is it a friendly greeting, eye contact, shake of the hand, offer to take a seat or offer a glass of water, tea or coffee? Will you want visitors to be escorted to the person they have an appointment with? Be clear about the ideal welcome you'd like your team to offer.
- Does everyone in your team notice your customers and greet them?
- What can you do to be even better at being there for your customers throughout their whole experience?
- What do you plan to do?

Watch for the signals

This is an obvious step, one that most people do instinctively. However, there are also many people who do not. As service professionals, we notice the subtle messages the customers are sending to us, as this informs us how we can best respond. Watch their body language and take note as they speak. What are they saying and how are they saying it? What is their tone of voice? What messages are you getting? This is why the first step is so important. If we're not there for our customers, we can't gather this information to respond to their needs. Remember, 'World Class Service' is about placing the customer in the centre of everything you do, not just following the process that works for you.

When we pay attention to the customer's body language, we can gauge how we might approach them in a way that complements their needs. For example, if a customer has a confused or potential annoyed look on their face, you'd approach them calmly and with an element of concern, rather than bouncing with energy and positivity.

Here are a couple more examples to bring this to life:
- a smiley and happy customer, I'd greet with a big smile and probably a louder, positive tone, and say 'How are you this morning?'

or

- a worried customer, I'd greet calmly, in a quieter, softer and neutral facial expression, and say 'Good morning, how can I help?'

Consider the following facial expressions. How would you approach a customer who seems:
- sad?
- stern?
- neutral, calm?
- angry?

Of course, their tone of voice works in conjunction with their facial expression and body language. That will re-enforce the message they give you.

The same principle applies on the phone. You can sense the mood of the person by the tone of their voice. You can also sense their body language although you can't see them. Not everyone agrees with me on this, but I am sure it is the case. The best example I can give you is that you can tell if someone is smiling and sitting up straight when you talk to them on the phone. They sound alert and positive. Try this with family and friends. Predict how they are sitting and their facial expression when you next speak on the phone. This requires you to heighten your listening skills. Listen for huffs and puffs, when your customer may be uncertain and need additional information or reassurance. Listen for the assertive decision-making tones that indicate they wish to go ahead.

An appropriate approach to a customer, one that is aligned to their body language, gives credibility and a good basis to move forward.

Having a blanket approach to all customers does not make them feel exceptional or considered.

When you have the customer in front of you, there are additional signals that indicate what they might need. For example, if they are struggling with a child's pushchair, bags and toddler, I'm sure the adult would appreciate a spot of assistance. Offer by saying something along the lines of 'May I help you with that?' We shall pick this up again in the next step of 'ask'. Other examples are when people look lost, have luggage, might have mobility needs, etc.

Practise this, pay attention to people generally and consider when they may need assistance. Many people 'people watch' as a hobby. You will soon become expert when it comes to responding to your customers' needs.

Service experts watch their customer's every move to 'be there' for them. This is a skill that, when perfected, will give you some amazing results. When you respond to the needs of your customers throughout their experience, this builds on their confidence in you and your business.

Notes

CASE STUDY

The best and easiest example to bring this to life is in a restaurant environment. I think most of us have dined in restaurants and can relate to this. In most eateries, we are greeted, taken to our table and offered drinks. The food order is taken; drinks and food are served. However, what if we want or need something whilst sitting at our table? The first thing we do as customers is look up. This is the signal to the serving staff that the customer wants or needs something. I call this 'Meerkat Moments'; you can tell at a glance in a restaurant that someone needs some assistance. In a great restaurant, the serving staff are there straight away to address the customer's needs.

In the world of building contractors, maybe the signals are when the client scratches their head or covers their mouth. This is a potential indication that they are not sure about something, they're nervous or undecided. Or maybe they're tired!

Thinking about your business:
- What signals do your customers give that indicate they want or need some assistance?
- What can you do to ensure that you are 'being there', that you see the signal and attend to their needs in a timely manner?

Continuing with the restaurant experience, when you have the food you have ordered, often the serving staff come back to check that everything with your meal is alright. We need to challenge the purpose of doing this check. The reason for me saying this is that they don't often 'watch the signals' and will ask when you have just placed food in your mouth, leaving it difficult to respond. Or there are times when you are in deep conversation and the serving staff interrupts. Rude! In exceptional restaurants, the serving staff pick an appropriate time to approach the table with the intention of establishing if everything is alright early on in the meal, so that if it's not right, there is an opportunity to make any corrections or adjustments.

This indicates that the team wants to ensure their customer leaves feeling that they have received exactly what they wanted and needed, with the added bonus of possibly even exceeding their expectations.

CONSIDER:

- What do you do to check the satisfaction of your customers during their experience in your business?
- What would you like to do to build on what you already do?
- What signals need to be considered to ensure you pick the right time for the customer?

To close the restaurant experience, what happens when the customers ask for the bill? This can be the most painful part of the experience. There have been times when it seems easy to leave without paying. (I have never done this, just for your information). This has been at times when the food has been amazing and we've received super service, yet the restaurant doesn't seem too keen to receive payment. I'm sure many people leave without paying. Worrying! This is clearly not good for business. The timing is important. The more efficient you are at making it easy for customers to pay, the better.

Another example of this is in retail establishments, where there are big signs that say 'Pay here' and there is no-one there. This says to me 'Help yourself to what you want, we don't want paying for the items you have selected.' It also states 'We are not being there for you.' Supermarkets have allowed customers to serve themselves, so the pace at which customers can pay and go has improved. This goes back to what I've said earlier; make it easy for your customers to spend money.

CONSIDER:

- What service, systems or processes do you have in place to ensure your customers can pay their bills quickly and efficiently that works for them and your business?
- What will you do to make improvements?

Ask questions

This is all about asking appropriate questions with the purpose of gaining information that will assist you in meeting the needs of your customer.

I realise this is simple, yet it isn't always applied, which makes the service less effective and/or efficient. At this point, you have been present ('Be there') so you can be instant when greeting a customer and notice the signals that have given you information. 'Watching for the signals' will prepare you for choosing which questions will be appropriate for you to ask.

To bring this to life, here's an example of when I was hosting a mini event to thank some close friends and family who'd helped me in the early days of my business. I wanted the evening to be small but perfectly formed. I had selected a lovely boutique hotel, who has a roof terrace—ideal as it was mid-summer. I had booked a table, selected and arranged canapes and champagne. My husband and I arrived early as I had some goody bags for my guests. I asked the staff if, as the guests arrived from the lift, the champagne would arrive instantly with no time delay. They agreed. My guests arrived and the champagne and canapes were served. We enjoyed the night, yet I left disappointed. Having worked in hospitality all my life, I blamed myself. I hadn't told them when making the booking that I'd like the canapes to be served to the guests. What they did was place the canapes on the table for everyone to help themselves, and after the first glass of champagne we poured our own. This is not what I expected. I felt that I could easily have created this at home. After all, I was paying for service. The lesson for the person who took my reservation would be to ask an appropriate question that allows me as the customer to explain how I see this working. As customers, we have our ideal in our head, and the service professional simply needs to get us to talk through what this looks and feels like. By the way, if they had poured the champagne, I'm pretty sure we would have consumed more.

It's important to select the right questions that will lead to the information required. I'm sure you've heard of open and closed questions.

Closed questions are the ones where you'd get a 'yes' or 'no' response.

Open questions are the ones that will give you information and will allow the customer to give specific detailed responses. Questions such as:

- How may I help you?
- What brings you to (name of your city/town/village)?
- What brings you to (name of your business)?
- What can I help you with?
- What is the purpose of your visit?
- What brings you here today?
- What are your plans for today?
- What are you looking for?
- Who are you here to see?
- What are you celebrating?
- What is the special occasion?
- How is the project progressing so far?
- What are you hoping to achieve?
- How are you feeling?
- What are your thoughts about this?
- Tell me what your special day would look and feel like?
- What would your ideal outcome be?
- What are you striving to achieve?
- What is your budget?
- How much time do you have?

These questions give you the opportunity to respond appropriately, which leads into the next step' Respond'.

CONSIDER:

Consider some open questions aligned to your business which would get to the heart of your customers' requirements.

Capture these below:

Closed questions are equally as powerful to get to the point of what your customer wants and needs. As a reminder, these are the questions that will lead your customer to respond very simply with a 'yes' or 'no'. These are efficient and effective in the right context. For example, 'Would you like to place the order?' 'Would you like me to get that for you now?' This is clear communication and directs you to deliver appropriately.

Leading questions are very off-putting. Questions such as 'Is everything alright with you/your meal?', etc. Clearly the person asking the question is wanting a 'yes' in response. This indicates that the intention of the business is not to know if their customers are satisfied or not. This implies they are checking satisfaction as it's something they should do, without a real purpose in understanding how the customer's experience is progressing. It would be far better to say 'How is everything with your meal?' This encourages the customer to describe their experience, giving you the opportunity to make any corrections or prevent any situation escalating.

Listen to how the customer responds to your question.

If they state 'Yeah, it's OK' or 'Yes, it's fine' in a not so interested manner, you might want to ask a further question to understand how you can make it exceptional. OK and fine as a level of satisfaction is likely to lead to potential dissatisfaction. This is your golden opportunity to turn this situation around.

Questions are powerful mid-way through your customer's experience, ensuring that your customers leave when all their needs are addressed. It is important you have the opportunity to correct anything your customer may want or need whilst you can. When they are leaving, you have no chance to make any alterations or right any wrongs they may have encountered. This is applicable when face to face or on the phone. Of course, it depends on what is happening with your customer at that time, but their body language will indicate to you what is going on for them. The type of business you are in will also determine what kind of questions you might ask.

Here are some general examples which you may want to tweak for your team or business. Please bear in mind that anything said by your team would ideally sounds genuine and natural, not robotic:

- What are your thoughts so far?
- What else might I be able to assist with?
- May I offer you...?
- What concerns do you have?

- What can I do to make this memorable for you?
- If there was one additional thing we'd need to consider to ensure all your needs are met, what would it be?
- What questions do you have for me?
- Who else might we need to consider?
- Would you be interested in...? (Only ask this kind of question once. If you have two things to offer, state this in one question, i.e. Would you be interested in life and home insurance?)

Listen

Listening is a skill that seems to be practised less and less. I'm not sure the reason for this. Although I think it may be because we believe we don't have the time to stop and pay attention to what is being said. Our minds are too busy having our own internal conversation, so when we do actually listen, we place our own take on what the other person is saying. To bring this to life, I recall a colleague who arrived into work as I was already sat in my office working away. When she arrived, she said 'Hi' followed by 'How was your weekend?' I turned to answer her question to realise she had moved into her own office with no intention of listening to my response. Her mind was clearly focused on what she was doing.

If you don't want to hear the answer, don't ask a question. This often happens when people say 'How are you?' whilst walking past then they don't wait to hear the answer.

When you want to offer a service to your customer that is exceptional, listening is vital to your success.

Ask a question with a genuine interest in gaining the response, along with wanting to hear the information you will gain.

This is a skill that many people find tricky. To fully listen to a customer with the intention of understanding takes focus. This leads to the listener having the ability to recite what they have understood to the customer. Stephen Covey describes this in *The 7 Habits of Highly Effective People*. Habit 4 is 'Seek first to understand, then to be understood', with next the habit being exactly where we want our service to be—Think win-win. The only way you can prove that you have heard and understood what someone else has said is by reflecting back your understanding. Only saying 'Yes, I understand' does not prove your understanding. The customer would have no clue what you have understood and will have no idea whether you will deliver aligned to their requirements or not.

Reflecting is summarising what your customer has said, like this:

Customer: 'May I have quote for the work to be done, one with the additional labour for the extension, a separate quote without the extension and a quote that shows just the materials?'

Service Professional: 'You're wanting 3 quotes, the whole job with labour, extension costs just with labour and one for just materials?'

Customer: 'Yes, that's exactly it.'

When you have listened carefully and are able to reflect back, this gives the customer reassurance that what they have asked for is likely to be delivered. It proves that the service professional has 'got it' in their own words and knows what is required. It also stops errors from being made so you get it right first time. This skill is what will set you apart from other service providers. When you have reached the 'yes' from the customer, you might want to gain clarification around other areas from your perspective or that of the customer. You may want to ask 'Is there anything else I need to consider?' That's another super question to gather more information.

In order to listen, we need to be fully present with the customer.

This means eye contact, observing their body language, and paying attention to their tone of voice. This is also the case on the phone, as already mentioned. Ensure your mind is with them and not wandering off into trying to interrupt what they are saying or placing your own story on theirs. It's about being totally with them, with an open mind. When you do this, you will be able to listen to what is not said. When you listen at this level you will notice body language and tone that may indicate that this is important to the client, or they are worried. You can then reflect to them, 'I'm getting the impression this is important to you.'

When you get it right, the customer often feels relieved. If you don't get it right, it still has the same effect, as the customer will correct you, and they're likely to respond with something like 'It's not important to me, it's more important to my boss/wife' or whatever they need to say. This will give you additional information that you can consider when delivering what the customer wants or needs. This is the greatest gift you can possibly give to your client.

This happens often when you dine in a restaurant and the serving staff take your order, then reflect back the order. This is to make sure they have everything. This gives them and you reassurance that the whole order is right and the side order hasn't been forgotten, or if it has, you have the opportunity to correct them, rather than being disappointed when your meal is served incomplete.

It also happens in many coffee shops when they take the order, then pass it over to the barista. You know you'll have the exact coffee that you've ordered— even if your name is not always the right spelling on the cup!

Overall, the objective is to listen with the intention of getting it right first time. Correct any misunderstanding sooner rather than later.

Reflecting doesn't have to be long-winded. Short and concise works. In the butchers, simply say '500kg of beef?' Customer: 'Yes'. It gives you the opportunity to differentiate between this customer and the last one. You're busy with many customers, all wanting similar things, yet the customer needs and wants to feel as though they are the first customer you've had, or at least you are giving them your undivided attention.

Notes

CASE STUDY

Here's an example from a customer of mine. We met for coffee to discuss what was going on in their business and which programme they wanted to support their team. The conversation was free flowing. I would reflect my understanding at certain points, they would correct me if I hadn't quite understood. This led to further explanation, giving me more important information. I gained a good insight into their business and their business needs. As a result of this conversation, I drafted a proposal to the client which was aligned to their objectives. The customer responded with 'How did you manage to get this to exactly what we wanted?' The secret is, I listened. It is effective and efficient to listen with the absolute intention of understanding the customer. Have a go and see what happens. After all, this is about delivering the needs of the customer.

On reflection from this, consider:
- Had you been the client in this example, how would you be feeling?
- As the client, what would you have been thinking?

Before thinking about your business, here are a few of my thoughts:
- Taking the time at the beginning saves time in the long term.
- Listening carefully, collecting all the detail, leads to being efficient and effective.
- Listening builds trust.

Thinking about your business:
- How do you and your team clarify the needs of your customers or clients to assure them what they want and need is what's going to be delivered?
- If they do, what impact is this having on your team and your customers?
- If they don't, what adjustments do you want to make? What impact will this have on the overall experience for your customer, team and business?

A small note to clarify; it is important that you know whether you can deliver the needs of the customer. If their needs are not aligned to what your business is about, then it is worth being honest and potentially recommending an appropriate alternative service provider. This will also win loyal customers for your future.

Respond

Having reflected your understanding of what the customer has requested, you will have already responded to a certain extent. However, this is also demonstrating that you have listened. When you have fully understood what the customer is asking for, you can respond in the most effective and efficient way, aligned to exactly what they have said. The key with your response is to be honest and to be clear about what is doable within realistic timelines. I realise there are many customers who have expectations which are crazy, but this is why understanding your customers and the market helps you to prepare for their potentially demanding requirements.

If you want to delight your customers, the key to how you and your team respond needs to be positive. Treat customers as though they are the first and only customer you have seen. Welcome and respond to them with a genuine smile, delighted to see them. This will form a whole new relationship with each individual customer.

Being positive is focusing on all that CAN be done, with little or no reference to what can't be done. Then deliver on that promise.

It is vital to do as you say you will, as this builds trust between you and your customer.

We are customers mainly because either we wish to buy an item, or we want or need a specialist skill or expertise. The key here is we, as the general public, are not the experts in everything. We touched upon this earlier. If jargon is used during conversations, we may as well have studied in the subject matter so we can understand, and if we had, their services would not be required.

A banking example: a mortgage advisor gives you the option that you could have a 'tracker mortgage'. What is one of those? The trick is to be able to explain to the customer what the options are or what needs to happen for you to be able to deliver exactly what the customer desires. Ensure your customer leaves feeling confident with any decisions or choices they have made.

Let's consider car mechanics: this is what I have experienced over the years. Clearly, I take the car because I've noticed a light come on the dash or there's a strange knocking as I drive. I pull up to the garage. The mechanic examines the car, then returns with a concerned look on his face. This makes me think this is the end of my car or a big bill is coming my way. He continues by sucking his teeth, shaking his head, then tells me, 'The (some strange name) of the shaft has blown, blah, blah, blah, (explaining all the ins and outs of how this shaft is connected to that shaft that makes the car run) blah, blah, blah.' This goes right over my head. I still have no clue! It all seems doom and gloom. It would be much better if he said in a calm tone, 'The (something) shaft has blown, which means you have three options: 1. I can research for a second-hand replacement, that will take a week to source and then fit, 2. Order a new one, that can be delivered and fitted by tomorrow or 3. Make a temporary fix now, with the chance it will go again in the near future.' Of course, he has a rough idea of costs too. At least this way I have a choice and solutions, these two being really important and much more reassuring to the customer.

When the request is straightforward, respond with doing what was requested. How you react is also important.

Responding positively means doing what is required with confident energy and focus, using upbeat and helpful language such as 'I shall get it for you,' or 'Certainly'.

There are many industries, such as solicitors, accountants, banks, estate agents, some health services, government departments or agencies who seem to consistently take their time in getting things done. With these industries, some things we know will take months to complete, yet in other parts of the world these things happen much more efficiently. I often wonder why these experts can't make changes and be far more customer focused and turn cases or projects around in a timely fashion. For example, reducing the length of time it takes in England to purchase a house to two weeks. How amazing would that be?

There is nothing worse than someone saying 'Yeah, sure, I'll get it', or maybe 'I'll try to do it today', then seeming to walk in slow motion, round-shouldered and sloppy. This is not exceptional; this is less than average, where the basics have not been embedded within the team and not satisfying what the customer needs at all, which is to feel confident and reassured that their needs will be met.

Responding might mean offering options for the customer based on the information they have given you. Wherever possible, offer your customer choice, we all love it.

If you need more information, ask more questions and listen so you can respond with all the information you need in order to be exceptional.

Always respond honestly. Don't say you will do something and then not. There's an expression, 'under promise and over deliver.' This is much better than the opposite, 'over promise and under deliver.' However, to be exceptional you would deliver exactly what you say you will in the time stated. This builds trust and loyalty where your customers know precisely what is happening and when.

To put this into context, here's a hotel example. When a guest (customer) orders food to their room, generally speaking, the guest will phone Room Service, place their order and a little while later the food is delivered to the guest's bedroom door. Sometimes the person taking the order for the guest will state that the food will be with the guest in 30 minutes. The guest may then decide to make good use of that time and jump into the shower. What if the food then arrived early—under promise, over deliver? The Room Service person might think this is good for the customer. However, it's not as they are now dripping wet and not quite ready to eat! Alternatively, the guest thinks 'great, half an hour, this will mean I can eat and leave just in time to meet my friends.' If the Room Service is later than stated, you have an agitated and annoyed guest when you deliver the food. Should no time be given and the guest asks 'How long will it take?', this is a sign that it's important to them. Whatever time you state, you need to deliver on time.

CONSIDER:

- How do you and your team respond to your customers?
- Do you and your team use positive language and body language when responding to your customers' needs?
- Do you respond using language your customer understands?
- Do you deliver within the times that you have stated?
- Are you honest when you respond to your customer?

Make it Memorable

Build on the whole experience at the greatest level. In order to do this, you need to remember! Remember the information you have gathered from your customer during their time with you. This shows that you have paid attention to what they have said. This also shows that you offer a personalised service, rather than processing your customers by saying the exact same thing to each one.

It's about giving your customer more thought and consideration than they had anticipated.

Up to now we have established the basics for our customers and considered and delivered their individual needs. Now we shall follow up in a way which demonstrates that you've taken the time to fully understand your 'one' customer who is with you in this moment, making the experience memorable.

To do this is often simple and costs nothing as it's about the generous spirit of the people providing the service. Here are some examples to get in this mindset:

In a clothing store: Where you have already assisted a customer when they went to try on a few clothing items and they come to pay. You may make a positive comment such as 'Ah, you went with the blue one, it looked great on you.'

In a supermarket: Where the customer is paying a cashier. You notice an item that you particularly like. You may make a positive comment such as 'Have you tried these before?', get the response from the customer, then follow up with 'They're delicious!'

In any situation: Where you notice your customer looking smart and well presented. You might say 'I really like your jacket, it's very smart.'

In a solicitor's office: Where the client has explained they're having many sleepless nights worrying about leaving their partner. You might say 'We shall get this on the way so you can sleep well at night, knowing your divorce is moving in the right direction.'

Any situation: When you recognise a customer from a previous visit or appointment. Depending on the situation, you may say 'Good morning, it's good to see you again.' Maybe 'Welcome back, how are you today?' If you can remember their name, this is even better—use it. There is nothing more personal than someone using your name. Use their name in a way that is suitable for your business. For example, in formal surroundings or businesses such as a solicitor, using the title of a customer would be appropriate, i.e. Mr, Mrs, Dr, Sir. In a coffee shop or car mechanics, the first name may be more appropriate.

This will depend on the customer too. The best thing to do if you are unsure is ask them.

Having asked questions to get to know your customer, they might reveal information that provides an opportunity for you to help them even further.

CONSIDER:

You arrive in a city you are visiting with the aim of seeing a certain landmark. The restaurant/shop/hotel/coffee shop you step into may apply the 6 steps to being exceptional and make conversation with you by asking you questions about your visit, which leads them to discover more about your likes and dislikes. They assist you with what you want and/or need in their business. They then write the name of a place that might interest you, along with its website. They say to you, 'I thought you might be interested in knowing about [place/restaurant/hidden treasure] while you're here. Have a good time.'

On reflection, consider:

- How would you respond to this?
- What would you be thinking?
- How would you feel?

It's not easy to prescribe 'make it memorable', as what you might do with your customers is personal to the customer with their unique individual needs, hence 'being exceptional'. It's not a process and not basic, yet it is easy to do—if you want to.

It's about your team having a desire to be exceptional in what they do, to be generous 'of spirit'.

Why not help people, rather than make life difficult for your customers?

In many professional services, remembering the customer's name, remembering what is unique about them, and what is important to them can easily be done. Remembering the names of their family, friends, pets or where they are visiting, where they plan to go on holiday, all show that you have listened and taken note about them as an individual, and it makes the customer feel that you care.

I worked with a bar person who was renowned at our hotel for remembering the drinks people had ordered months previously when they last visited. Madge was a legend in her own time. Most of the customers knew her. The service she offered was direct and to the point. She'd approach the customers at their table and suggest another round of drinks. She'd remember their order and simply serve them again. It was quick, efficient and the customers loved her. She made it easy for the customers to spend money. She knew when to have a chat with them and when not to. Of course, when Madge was on duty, sales were up. Everyone who looks after customers has opportunities each and every day to shine and build their legacy. Just like Madge did. With exceptional service, everyone wins.

It can be very powerful, especially when people don't expect the added extras.

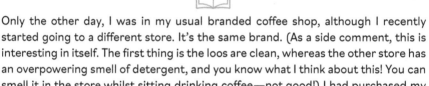

Only the other day, I was in my usual branded coffee shop, although I recently started going to a different store. It's the same brand. (As a side comment, this is interesting in itself. The first thing is the loos are clean, whereas the other store has an overpowering smell of detergent, and you know what I think about this! You can smell it in the store whilst sitting drinking coffee—not good!) I had purchased my coffee from a serving assistant who was smiley, friendly and polite. I sat for a while writing, then got up to leave. She said, 'Thank you, have a great day.' My reaction: 'Wow!' I left with a warm, fuzzy feeling, knowing I was valued and acknowledged. They don't normally even pay attention to people leaving the store.

All of this applies to any industry—solicitors, builders, plumbers, electricians, joiners, banking, financial services, teachers, personal trainers, doctors, nurses, surgeons, restaurants, shops, hotels, online retailers, travel agents, car rental—and the list can go on and on. Wherever there is a customer, someone paying or benefiting from your organisation or business, it is applicable. The mindset is: What is important to this customer? How can I make this memorable for them today?

In order to bring the *6 Steps to Exceptional Service* together, I have two examples where following the 6 steps would potentially have changed the whole experience.

The first example is in a premium car showroom:
A friend was having their car serviced. Whilst they were booking the car in, I thought I'd have a look at the fancy, shiny new cars. The basics in the showroom were super: the cars looked good, the car salespeople were well presented, it smelt fresh and aired, and the style of cars were to my taste. I wandered amongst the

different style of cars, such as 4x4, family saloon, 2-seater sports cars. I was just looking in the window of a family saloon car when the salesperson approached me. He was very friendly and knowledgeable. He said 'Good morning', then told me all the facts about the car. It was impressive: speed, fuel consumption, safety features were all recited to me. I thanked him. However, I felt overwhelmed with a whole pile of information that didn't mean very much to me, so I didn't know how to respond. I was only browsing! I left the showroom with no connection to the brand or with any desire to consider this brand in the future.

I'm sure you have many ideas of what could have happened. Had he followed the *6 Steps to Exceptional Service* it might have looked like this:

Be there: Be available to interact with the customers—he was there.

Watch the signals: They would see that there's a browsing potential customer in the store (perfect, so much money is spent on the brand to get people into the business). The browsing customer has just come in with an existing customer, so maybe they like their car and might have persuaded their friend or relative into wanting one of the cars. What do they seem to be interested in? Are they aiming for a certain car or are they looking at all cars? He might have done this, but I don't know what information he gathered from how I behaved.

Ask questions: This is where this person missed the point. He launched into telling me! He didn't at any stage place me in the centre of the experience. He could have asked, 'What brings you here today?' I would have responded about my friend and his car being serviced. He could have followed up with, 'If you were interested in any car, which would it be?'

Listen: My response would have been 'A sports car with a black interior and a good music system.' He could have clarified his understanding with 'Ah, a sporty car'. To which I would have said something like 'Yes, ideally with four seats.'

Respond: This would have given him an opportunity to take me over to the sporty cars, allow me to sit in it, ask me what I thought, show the music system, and explain the options of interiors. He might have asked further questions, such as 'What do you think?' I'm pretty sure I would have loved it.

Make it memorable: There are many things that could have happened here. Maybe he could have asked if I had the time and offer me a test drive. I realise this might not always be practical, however on the off-chance when it is doable, do it. It would 'WOW' the customer and definitely make it memorable. Maybe offer me a brochure with his name and number on it. The latter would have been more appropriate for me, as my friend by this time would have booked his car in and would be waiting for me. I would have left the showroom with information that would have left me with the desire to potentially want one of their cars at some point in the future, or even then with a choice that would have made it easy for me to buy. If I had driven the car and gained a feel for it, I probably would be so excited and wanted to have the car.

Notice the key stages where he missed the opportunity. Had he asked the question relating to me, this would have given the opportunity to align his knowledge to my needs. This would have been exceptional.

The second example is a hotel:

At 8am I entered a beautiful hotel. The arrival experience was lovely, with all the basics in place: the gardens were in full bloom, looking very pretty, no weeds, no litter; the entrance was clean and tidy, well-presented people welcoming their customers, the glass door gleaming with no streaks, fingerprints or drips; the smell through the gardens and into the entrance of the hotel was gorgeous; all the seating had plumped up cushions and a gentle aroma of freshly brewed coffee. I was pulling my overnight rolling case. The doorman opened the door, welcomed me into the hotel, and a porter was there instantly, anticipating the arrival of his customers. He greeted me with 'Will you be staying with us tonight?' I responded with 'No'. He then asked, 'Would you like to leave your luggage with us?' I responded with 'No'. I explained to him that I was to meet a colleague who was hosting a meeting in the hotel and that I'd need my luggage with me for my laptop, papers, etc. He then asked, 'What is the name of the company the meeting might be under?' I explained. He then directed me to the room. That was it. We got there after 3 questions—not bad. However, to be effective, efficient and exceptional, this might be how this could have been replayed:

Be there: The doorman and porter where there, opened the door and instant welcome. Great.

Watch the signals: The porter responded to me by acknowledging the luggage I was pulling. Brilliant.

Ask questions: Had he asked 'What brings you to the hotel today? He would have got to the heart of my needs instantly.

Listen: I would have responded with 'I have a meeting with a specified company'. Maybe I could have said 'And I'm running late' (I wasn't). He could have clarified the name of the company, and this would have reassured me that he had the right company and I wasn't going to be sent to the wrong room and potentially been embarrassed.

Respond: He could have then directed me to the right room, and if late, with pace. He might have asked another question: 'Will you be needing your luggage with you?'

Make it memorable: He might have said, 'Let me take you to the room and take your luggage for you.' This would have taken the stress of finding the room away and given me a moment to think about the meeting, rather than following directions to the room. I would feel a sense of calm, relaxed and cared for. Isn't this what we want for our customers? This porter might have seen me after the meeting, and to make it even more memorable might have followed up with 'How did your meeting go?' and so, the *6 steps to exceptional* could start again. He could have assisted me with my next meeting locally. Who knows? It's all circumstantial.

It might be that you cannot always make it memorable for every customer as this might be impossible or not required. For example, I may want to go into a shop and buy one item and leave. The shop assistant, when watching the signals, will know that to purchase the item is all that is required. However, to be polite and thank the customer is a basic.

Challenge yourself and your team to strive to make it memorable for one customer per day. Practise this so that you and your team naturally look for memorable opportunities and it becomes a way of life. One a day will start taking steps to upgrading your customer experience. Build a reputation of being exceptional and be confidently ahead of your competitors.

All organisations can make this happen if everyone in the organisation is aligned to the aspiration of the business owner. It's heart-warming to see more independent stores placing the customer at the centre of all they do. This is doable in larger organisations too. I think the owners and CEO's think the service is being provided, yet the reality is it's not.

Taking your experience to exceptional levels

Having completed the 'Feel' chapter, you have completed your first draft of your *10-Service Standards Checklist*, which is aligned to the standards you would like to be delivered consistently throughout your business. Ideally, it will take three to six months for your team to have mastered the delivery of these initial sensory standards. When you are satisfied that these are entrenched within your team, you can introduce your second *10-Service Standards Checklist*, focusing on one customer at a time to create exceptional service.

You can compile this second *Service Standards Checklist* now so that it is ready to go when you and your team are ready. This takes you further in placing your customer at the centre of all you and your team do. You can now develop your second *Service Standards Checklist* to include some of the exceptional behaviours you'd like your customers to experience throughout their time with you.

The overall objective is to make it clear for you and your team to know what exceptional looks and feels like.

The only way to embed exceptional service constantly and consistently is to measure against the service standards, making this a natural way of working. You will upgrade and review the *10-Service Standards Checklist* to ensure the sensory and emotional standards are continually kept alive. As mentioned a number of times throughout the book, this should be as routine as how you monitor your financial results, a normal way of examining how your business is doing.

Here are some examples for each of the *6 Steps to Exceptional Service* that you may want to include in your next *Service Standards Checklist* when the basics have been achieved. You might want to blend some of the sensory basics. Remember, these need to be considered at every stage of your customer experience: at the beginning, middle and end.

6 STEPS TO EXCEPTIONAL SERVICE STANDARDS:

Be there

Consider these throughout your customer experience:

Are you and your team physically there/present to greet and acknowledge each and every customer?	Y☐	N☐
Are you and your team mentally there/present to observe and fully engage, to consider what your customers may want or need throughout?	Y☐	N☐
Are you and your team looking up in anticipation for customers arriving into your business or your area of the business?	Y☐	Y☐
Do you or your team notice the arrival of a customer and open the door to your premises as they arrive?	Y☐	N☐
Are you and your team ready to accept payment when the customer is ready?	Y☐	N☐
Are you and your team present as the customer needs additional assistance?	Y☐	N☐
Is there always one of your team present whilst a customer is present?	Y☐	N☐
Do you and your team acknowledge each and every customer in a positive manner that indicates that you are there for them? i.e. a smile, a nod of the head, a good morning	Y☐	N☐
Do you and your team answer the phone within 3 rings?	Y☐	N☐
Are you and your team attentive and focused only on the customer whilst on the phone?	Y☐	N☐

Watch the signals

Consider these throughout your customer experience:

Do you and your team switch your behaviour to meet the needs of the customer? When the customer is looking happy, you welcome them positively. If they look concerned or serious, you welcome them with a calm tone. Y ☐   N ☐

Do you and your team offer assistance where it is clear the customer is needing additional help? i.e. notice their body language. Y ☐   N ☐

Do your customers receive instant assistance? i.e. within 3 seconds. Y ☐   N ☐

Do you and your team notice the behavioural needs of your customer when on the phone? Do you change your approach aligned to the differing behaviours of the customer? e.g. happy, calm, serious, etc. Y ☐   N ☐

Ask questions

Consider these throughout your customer experience:

Do you and your team ask questions to gather information so you can instantly offer the appropriate assistance to your customers when they enter your business? e.g. How may I help you? What brings you to (name of the business) today? Y ☐   N ☐

Do you and your team ask questions to gather information so you can instantly offer the appropriate assistance to your customers when they phone your business? e.g. How may I help you? Y ☐   N ☐

Do you and your team ask questions during the customer's experience within your business to establish if they want or need any additional support, information, service? Y ☐   N ☐

Do you and your team ask questions to gain further information from your customers, to ensure customers get all they may want and need? Ensuring that the customer receives the best experience possible. Y ☐   N ☐

Do you and your team ask questions during the customer's time in your business to gather information with the intention of establishing if the customer is satisfied with their experience so far, so appropriate adjustments can be made to make their experience exceptional? Y ☐   N ☐

Do you and your team ask your customers their level of satisfaction as they are about to leave your business? Y ☐   N ☐

Do you and your team ask your customer questions to understand how you could have made their experience even better? Y ☐   N ☐

Listen

Consider these throughout your customer experience:

Do you and your team show active listening skills when interacting with customers and each other? i.e. stop what you are doing, look at the other person and seem genuinely interested in what is being said and wait for them to finish before making any comment.　Y ☐　N ☐

Do you and your team reflect back your understanding to ensure you have heard the right information to assist your customers?　Y ☐　N ☐

Are you and your team totally focused on the caller when on the phone? i.e. not distracted by looking at computer screens or any other distractions.　Y ☐　N ☐

Do you and your team listen intently whilst on the phone with your customers? Ensuring you are focused entirely on the customer.　Y ☐　N ☐

Respond

Consider these throughout your customer experience:

Do you and your team respond positively to the information received from your customers? e.g. say 'Certainly', 'Yes, of course I shall get this for you now.' 'Let me check this for you.'　Y ☐　N ☐

Do you and your team show positive body language in response to the information you receive from your customers? e.g. smile, or with a sense of urgency.　Y ☐　N ☐

Do you and your team respond with what is possible to assist your customers? Giving them options and honest information.　Y ☐　N ☐

Do you and your team respond using language that will be understood by all customers? i.e. free from expert terminology or jargon that might not be understood by others.　Y ☐　N ☐

Do you and your team respond positively, making realistic commitments to your customers?　Y ☐　N ☐

Do you and your team respond positively to your customers' requests when on the phone?　Y ☐　N ☐

Do you and your team have professional body language and a tone of voice that demonstrates attentive behaviour when speaking with your customers?　Y ☐　N ☐

Make it memorable

Consider these throughout your customer experience:

Do you and your team actively seek opportunities to create a memorable experience for your customers?　Y ☐　N ☐

	Y	N
Do you and your team make a personal connection with your customers?	☐	☐
Do you and your team ensure your customers leave your business with a genuine and personalised farewell?	☐	☐
Do you and your team naturally use the customer's name when known?	☐	☐
Do you and your team work together to share any information you have learned about the customer, so this can be used throughout other areas of the customer experience?	☐	☐
Do you and your team use conversation to gather more information from your customers so you can make use of this information in order to make their experience memorable? e.g. special occasions, planned holidays, the well-being of their relative, etc.	☐	☐
Do you and your team use conversation to gather the maximum amount of information from your customers on the phone so you can share this with the rest of the team to make the customer experience memorable?	☐	☐

Which of these do you already do consistently?

Celebrate what you notice you and your team do well. Encourage them to maintain this consistently. Share what you have noticed with your team, so they are likely to continue to create that feel-good factor and high standards in your business.

Create your second *Service Standards Checklist* to embed the *6 Steps to Exceptional Service* with your customers, at every opportunity, one customer at a time.

Your upgraded *Service Standards Checklist* may look something like this:

	SERVICE STANDARDS CHECKLIST	YES/NO
1	**Do colleagues actively welcome customers into the business? Open the door for customers when they can?** *(Be there)*	No
	What did you observe/notice?	
	James was looking at the computer as the customer entered the building.	
2	**Did the colleague look genuinely pleased to see the customer?** *(Be there)*	Yes
	What did you observe/notice?	
	When James looked up (about 10 seconds after the customer had arrived), he smiled at them with a sparkle in his eye that looked genuine.	
3	**Did the colleague ask a question to establish how they could best assist the customer?** *(Ask questions)*	Yes
	What did you observe/notice?	
	James said, 'Good afternoon, what can I help you with today?'	
4	**Does the environment look and feel clean, fresh and well presented?** *(See)*	Yes
	What did you observe/notice?	
	All surfaces clean and free from dust or debris. Smelt clean, fresh and aired. All literature on display for the customers' use was well presented, free from rips, tears and graffiti.	
5	**Do the colleagues listen carefully when the customer is speaking to them?** *(Listen)*	No
	What did you observe/notice?	
	James was looking at the computer when the customer was giving them their name.	
6	**Do the colleagues respond positively to the requests made by the customer?** *(Respond)*	Yes
	What did you observe/notice?	
	James nodded his head, smiled, said, "I will call Jerry to let him know that you are here."	
7	**Do colleagues acknowledge or offer to assist customers whilst in the business?** *(Be there & watch the signals)*	Yes
	What did you observe/notice?	
	Harry walked through the corridors and looked at a customer walking past him. He smiled at them and said 'Good afternoon.'	
8	**Do all customers show positive language and body language when interacting with customers and each other?** *(Respond)*	No
	What did you observe/notice?	
	Colleagues ignored each other when moving around the business.	

SERVICE STANDARDS CHECKLIST		YES/ NO
9	**Do colleagues personalise the farewell to customers as they leave your business?** *(Make it memorable)*	Yes
	What did you observe/notice? As a customer left, James said, 'It was good to meet you, Mr Thompson, I look forward to seeing you again soon. Enjoy the rest of your day.'	
10	**Are all your toilet facilities well presented, smelling clean, fresh and aired?** *(See & smell)*	No
	What did you observe/notice? No toilet paper in one cubicle. Excess amount of water around the sink area. Smells stale.	
Total: **Comments/What have you learned?**		*6/10* *=60%*

Creating an exceptional emotional connection with your customers requires everyone to place them at the centre of everything you do. When you gather all relevant information from your customer you have a good chance to make their experience memorable, which will capture their hearts and minds. This is when your business will stand out from your competition.

Trust and loyalty are likely to lead to your customer proactively promoting your business, and this is the key to an ongoing successful business. As long as complacency doesn't step in and monitoring your customers' satisfaction is at the heart of everything you and your team do, you will remain on the right track.

In reality, there will be times when things don't go to plan, or the customers' expectations are not met. It is important that everyone in the team has the drive and desire to understand what went wrong with the intention of continually improving. The next chapter will assist in building confidence to deal with any kind of negative comments from customers.

STAGE 3.
BE CONFIDENT

Embrace feedback and be confident
in your response when a customer
is dissatisfied.

9

WHAT IF...
IT DOESN'T GO
AS WE INTENDED?

U p to now we have talked about getting it right and even getting it exceptional...but with the best will in the world, things sometimes go wrong. What matters is how you deal with it.

We have explored what being exceptional looks and feels like and how to respond. During the delivery of a service, it's important to make it easy for customers to say if the experience they are having is not as they expect. You do not want them telling everyone apart from you, especially with the power of social media. One not-so-good experience shared can soon spread like a virus to ruin your business's reputation.

The minute you become complacent and think you have it all right is the minute your business is likely to fail.

The fact is, there will be customers who have expectations of your product and/or service that are not met. As long as you have the intention of wanting to hear about this and do something about it you can continue your journey to an on-going, buoyant business.

Here are some statistics that highlight why handling complaints well is so important to your business success:

Statistics

- Organisations never hear from 96% of their unhappy customers
- A dissatisfied customer may tell 9-10 people
- For every complaint received, there are 26 customers with similar concerns
- 70% of complainants will do business with you again if the matter is resolved effectively, 95% if the complaint is resolved quickly
- Customers who have their complaints satisfactorily resolved tell 5 people
- It costs 5 times as much to attract a new customer than an existing customer

Taken from People 1st, World Host Principles of Customer Service

I realise that there are many who believe that there are professional complainers out there. This might be true. However, if we choose to place them in the category of 'professional complainers' and don't give them our full attention, we've lost—not only a potential loyal customer, but the whole reputation or perception of the business, of caring and showing that there is a genuine desire to want to know if something is not as the customer had expected. I've yet to establish what professional complainers look and sound like. I personally wouldn't take the risk of spending too much time thinking about it. I'd much rather treat every single customer with the respect and integrity aligned to me and my business aspirations.

Do we truly pay attention to what people have got to say? We have to treat every person with the absolute intention of fully understanding what they are telling us and respond to their comments.

Your customer's opinion on their experience is critical information.

You gain a different perspective which you may not have considered. This information may inspire a new product or service which has the potential to improve your business and challenge you and your team to constantly think:

What can we do to be even better?

Mindset and behaviours

Having a guide or procedure within your organisation is important so everyone knows where they stand, so that each staff member is responsible and knows how they should act. A procedure that is based on listening, reflecting your understanding, thanking the customer for their feedback, genuinely apologising, asking for suitable solutions that are right for them, considering their suggestion and following up to ensure it has been done ensures they are happy. This will assist you and your team in having a consistent approach when dealing with all customers.

For example—a hotel one—we created a culture of doing the right thing for the customer within reason. The team would assess the situation and agree how to resolve the issue with the customer. They all knew that they would be supported with their decision. There wasn't a time when the team overcompensated, like agreeing to a free stay as a result of the customer not receiving their morning newspaper.

If you haven't got a procedure, encourage management to create one. If this doesn't happen, it is still possible for you to follow the 6 steps independently. This is explained further within this chapter.

The skill of asking the right questions and listening very carefully to the answer with the intention of fully understanding what the customer is saying and feeling is critical. Every single person who is interacting with your customers is in a prime position to gather information about your customers' responses and what they are telling you about their experience. How often do you ask your team what they have learned from the customers that day? Do you ever ask, 'What could we do to make our product or service even better?'

There will be some people in your team who already share this information and would be willing to gather it. Also, there will be many who feel less comfortable with this idea, for various reasons. There will be people who are confident in dealing with disgruntled customers and those less so. By having a robust system in place, it helps all members of staff to know how to deal with it and it makes them feel safe in sharing so that the company can collect all the information and learn. Past experience may have left them feeling apprehensive about how to deal with it. It could be that they then have been blamed for an issue that was beyond their control.

After all, everything we have done for our customer is with the intention of doing a good job. When a customer tells us it wasn't so good, it's like someone has burst our bubble. Our internal dialogue kicks in with phrases like 'We never meant to mess up', 'How did this go so wrong?', 'What do I do now?', 'I can't make this right when the damage is done', 'Help!', and 'Get the manager.' As this potential internal chat is going on, it is likely that our body language is reflecting this negativity—a facial expression full of doubt and/or fear, the shoulders, head and whole demeanour drops. This is being observed by the customer, which may give the impression that your team lacks self-confidence.

CONSIDER:

Consider how you respond when you are dissatisfied. Think about a time when you were not impressed with a product or service you received. What were you thinking? Maybe things like:

- This is not what I was expecting.
- I'm not impressed.
- I've been ripped off.
- They don't seem to care.
- This is important to me, etc.

As these thoughts are whizzing around your head, your emotions kick in (if they haven't already), which might leave you feeling:

- frustrated
- angry
- disappointed
- upset, etc.

How did you feel?

When we are in an emotional state, we behave in a way that is not our 'normal' level-thinking way. This manifests in different ways for different people. In my experience, I've had customers who:

- shout
- are rude
- swear
- tell me that I'm useless
- are very calm
- are demanding
- say nothing, yet their tone of voice might be dismissive

How did you behave?

What to remember is that the customer has their perception of what they expect and what 'good' looks like for them. We often don't know where they get this perspective from. It may be from a recommendation, from your website or having met someone who works within your team. No matter where they've gained this perspective, you need to know what it is, e.g. I expected this yet received only that. It is important to get this information so that you understand the expectation so the situation can be corrected, if possible.

The response is critical. I have seen colleagues behave in variations of the following:

- Roll their eyes at the customer as they repeat their story.
- Bow their head. (as though in shame)
- Get the manager as quickly as possible.
- Try to interrupt the customer.
- Question every detail of the complaint: What happened there? What time did that happen? Who did you speak to? (Interrogating the customer, almost as a witness to the crime!)
- Get frustrated with the customer who is going on and on and on.
- Say to them 'Thank you for letting us know. I'm sorry this happened.' (That's it)
- Giving an explanation of why it went wrong. Please note, this is not your customer's problem, so don't even try to explain.
- Sigh heavily...

...and so the list goes on.

Whilst the customer has their thoughts and feelings which direct their behaviour, the same is happening for us as service professionals.

CONSIDER:

Consider what thoughts you had as a service professional the last time a customer started to tell you what had happened. Here are some of my thoughts, along with those of others who have shared with me:

- Oh my goodness, here's another.
- What can I do for this customer? Maybe I can give them this? Or maybe that? What did we do for that complaint the other day? I'm not sure if I'm allowed to do this? I'll have to get my supervisor/manager. They're not in until later. Oh no!
- This person is a professional complainer, they're only after some money off.
- This is awful, we have really messed up. I feel really bad for them. How did we manage to mess up so badly? I'm embarrassed.
- This person is like a stuck record, they've just repeated the same point four times over, oh and there they go again, five times. What shall I have for dinner tonight? (drifting into your own thoughts whilst the customer continues with their story).
- I'm not sure how this happened. Who dealt with this? It seems that the company procedure wasn't followed. Someone has overlooked some important information.

What were your thoughts during your last interaction with a customer who was dissatisfied?

Just like the customers, what you are thinking creates an emotion for you. Here are the emotions some people have shared with me of how they feel as a service professional whilst the customers are expressing their concern:

- Disappointed
- Intimidated
- Afraid
- Anxious
- Upset
- Bored
- Frustrated
- Ashamed
- Nervous
- Embarrassed

These feelings then lead to how we might behave, as detailed previously, with our head bowed down, sighing, getting the manager, etc. This is what the customer is watching very closely, whilst in their emotional state.

Allow the customer all the time they need to express what they want and need to express. It's our job as service professionals to show that we have understood. This allows the customer to feel valued and understood, and not processed. Then search for suitable solutions in the most effective and efficient way to meet the needs of the customer—with them.

Remember your vision and intention

It is helpful if your organisation has guidelines of how they expect complaints to be handled, where to record the details of the complaint, along with any kind of compensation that might be considered or offered as suitable for varying situations. If this is not the case, then perhaps make this suggestion or keep a record yourself, so this can be monitored with the intention of understanding what is happening. This will give clarity on the cost and nature of complaints so you can learn, respond appropriately and make improvements.

Remain focussed on the outcome of a happy customer who feels valued and wants to return in the future and you will find it easier to come up with an acceptable solution. The only way you can do this is by responding to their personal needs. It's not an opportunity to express to the customer how you have made a mistake, or to say the situation is out of your hands. I've heard so many service professionals say 'I'm sorry about this, unfortunately we're short-staffed today, three people have phoned in sick.' The customer doesn't need to know, and they don't care. It's not their problem. This might be the case, but the only thing the customer cares about is them and what they wanted from your business. Applying a spot of guilt onto the customer is not going to help them, it's likely to frustrate them even more. Keep focused on the customer, not on you or your team's circumstances.

To flip the experience to be exceptional and create that emotional connection, you need to be confident in your intentions and show this through your body language, your tone of voice and the words that you use.

There are so many times that I have dealt with dissatisfied customers. Having no complaints is worrying. It is only practice that built my confidence so that I could engage with the customer in a way that would ensure that they left on a positive—most of the time.

Remember, these customers are going to keep coming—we hope! Without them, we would have no business. If we don't respond and encourage feedback, our customers will simply take their business elsewhere! By showing that you want and value your customers, you have them emotionally. It shows that everyone within your team is serious about service.

CONSIDER:

- Is everyone in your team keen to gain feedback, to learn from your customer so that you and your team become even better?
- What systems and processes do you have in place to learn from your customers?
- What is being said by your customers?
- What do you do to become even better?

Organisations that currently do this well see themselves as their biggest competitors. They have a mindset of 'our latest product or service experience is now out of date, what can we do to compete against ourselves so that we remain relevant to our customers, so they constantly want the new version of our product?'

CONSIDER:

Consider your business and how it is performing currently then answer the following questions:

The last service contract that you completed.

- What went well?
- What one or two things could have been done better that would make you stand out from your competitor?
- Were there any negative issues for the client? If so, what were they? What can be done to eliminate these in the future?
- What will you do?

Review the service delivery from the last shift or day.

- What went well?
- What one or two things could have been done better that would make you stand out from your competitor?
- Were there any negative issues for the customers? If so, what were they? What can be done to eliminate these in the future?
- What will you do?

Examine a product that doesn't sell well.

- What other product might complement it, so this product would sell?
- What is it that makes this product less appealing than others? Potentially ask one or two trusted loyal customers who might be able to help you.
- What might you replace this product with?
- What do your customers want or need instead? Again, potentially ask one or two loyal customers who might be able to help you.
- Were there any negative issues about this product? If so, what were they? What can be done to eliminate these in the future?
- What will you do?

Review the last case or project you've recently completed or even a project where you are part the way through.

- What timescales did you agree with your clients?
- How well did you deliver on those timescales?
- What was the ideal outcome for your client? Was this delivered or is it being delivered?
- What are the one or two things that could have been or can be done better that would make you stand out from your competitor?
- Were there any negative issues for the client? If so, what were they? What can be done to eliminate these in the future?
- What will you do?

Exceptional organisations constantly review and monitor so they challenge themselves to upgrade their offering on a daily, weekly, monthly, and/or annual basis. It takes drive, determination, time, focus and energy to do. I know, as I strive to constantly improve *Zest for Life* programmes! The critical element is to be honest with yourself. You are your biggest critic. If you want to be exceptional and know that you're not there yet, take a look through the standards explored in this book and take one or two steps forward. Then ensure you acknowledge your progress.

Whilst there's the critic in us all, there's also our ego that sits alongside it. If you convince yourself that you are doing the best job that you can and it IS exceptional, you could be closing yourself off from listening to your customers and team. The long-term impact of you believing that you are exceptional already, with no possibility of upgrading your product or service, will be loss of business.

Tricky people

It is difficult when the staff member doesn't know what to do or is not confident with a dissatisfied customer. (After all, as a staff member, it's not pleasant to hear how everything you do is no good or dealing with people being rude). What is important is that each colleague is clear about what their intention is. Do you recall the exercise you completed during the introduction? When asking people what their intention is when they come to work, each and every one has said something along the lines of 'Do a good job'. Whether this is true or not, I don't know. I can only give a view from the information given. We need to remind ourselves that every person in the team wants to do a good job. Keep this intention in mind as you communicate with the unhappy customer: the customer has chosen you to share their dissatisfaction. View this a golden opportunity to prove that you and your team are exceptional in everything you do. Your whole demeanour will mirror your intention and would be something like this:

Body language
- Eye contact, paying close attention to what the customer is saying and how they are saying it (watching their body language)
- Upright posture, standing straight
- Head up
- 100% focused on the customer

Consider what to say only when they have finished telling you about their experience and expectations. When they have finished, there will be a pause. This is your signal to reflect your understanding of the customer's dissatisfaction. Then ensure the other aspects of how you communicate with the customer is aligned to your body language:

Tone of Voice
- Calm
- Natural

Words
- To reflect their situation (as we talked about in 'Be exceptional', listen with the intention of understanding)

The 6 *Steps to Exceptional Service* can help to structure how this works, although in a slightly different order. This is how to do it:

Step 1: Be there

Be totally present with the customer as they express themselves. This is important to the customer, so it's important to you too. This time should be the one and only time the customer has to go through this information. To be exceptional we need to pay attention.

Remember, 70% of customers who have their complaint resolved effectively are likely to return. 95% of customers are likely to return when their complaint is resolved quickly and effectively.

With this information in mind, it is a golden opportunity to learn about their experience and have the potential to do something about it.

As you listen, strive to keep yourself in a calm state. Keep focused, attentive and breathe, so you can be the best version of yourself when you respond to the customer. This requires you to stop and be fully present.

Whilst someone is in an emotional state, they are behaving in a way that is not the true version of themselves. This emotional state can only be upheld by someone for a short period. For example, think about a time when you have laughed and laughed so much that it hurts. You laugh and then pause, take a breath and somehow gather yourself back to a calm and controlled state. We can't laugh all afternoon. It's the same with crying. No matter how sad the situation, we cry in short bursts, gather ourselves together then become calm again. We may return to laughter or crying if and when we are reminded of the situation, which results in another emotional outburst. This is exactly what is happening with our customers. They are angry in that moment, behaving in the way that is emotionally driven. As soon as they have expressed themselves, they then pause and gather themselves to be calm again. It is when they get to this pause and breathe that we are able to speak and not before. If we interrupt the customer whilst they are off-loading their situation, it will re-fuel their emotions and they are likely to take even longer to express themselves.

Simply let them say what they want and need to say. You need to 'be there' for them. Maintain eye contact, be still and calm and give them your full attention. To assist you in keeping calm and not taking anything they might say personally, here's my advice. I used to almost detach from the situation (whilst still listening intently), as though they were talking about someone else. Remember this is not the true version of themselves. You will soon have the calm version of this customer to talk things through.

Overall, what you want your customers to know is that you are serious about your product and service and you want to know when they are not happy. Surely you would rather the customer tell you first rather than telling other people and potentially the rest of the world via social media. You can only do this if you are there for them.

Step 2: Watch the signals

As they express themselves, pay full attention. Ideally you would empty your mind of other thoughts, so 100% of your attention is on them. Collect data which includes the words they are using—you might notice they use a specific word or phrase a number of times, such as 'I'm really annoyed', then carry on with their explanation. Take note of their body language: what do you notice? You may see that they are tapping on the table. What is their facial expression telling you? Ultimately what you're trying to do is imagine what it might be like if you were them.

Whilst you may not see their complaint as being so terrible, you also need to remember that you don't know what else might be happening in their lives. Why has this situation sparked such a reaction? What we do know is that this person had an expectation that was greater than what they received.

Here we switch the order of the *6 Steps* to:

Step 3: Listen

As I have highlighted previously, the only way we can demonstrate that we have listened effectively is by reflecting back what we have heard or understood.

Listen attentively until the customer has finished. Allow that pause to happen, give a second or two before you speak to make sure they have finished. In my experience, sometimes they carry on once they have taken a breath. When this happens, simply continue listening.

When the pause arrives, this is when you demonstrate to the customer that you have paid full attention to their overall message. You reflect back what you have understood about their dissatisfaction in one or two sentences. You may use one of their key words that they have repeated, such as 'I have the impression that we've not met your expectations and this has led to you being annoyed with your whole experience.' (You will choose the word 'annoyed' as they might have used this word several times as they talked through the situation. You might have noticed their body language seeming agitated and annoyed too.) They will respond with either 'Yes' or they may correct you with 'No, I'm frustrated more than annoyed.' You being right is not the point, the point is letting the customer know that you are trying to see the situation from their perspective. If you gain a 'yes' response or correction, more often than not you will notice the customer seems to become more relaxed. This is them moving out of their emotional state and is often when you can have a constructive conversation with them. There will always be exceptions to this pattern of behaviour. We are all individuals and don't always behave in a prescribed way.

Keep striving to understand. If the customer has responded with 'I'm feeling more frustrated than annoyed', then reflect back the word 'frustrated.' The customer will then give you the 'yes' that you are looking for.

Please note that saying 'I understand' to a customer is NOT demonstrating that you understand or that you've heard them. How could you? You have no idea what is going on in all aspects of their life which has caused them to be so frustrated about this situation. You might think, 'If this happened to me, I think I would be angry too' or 'I had a similar experience that happened to me like this and it wasn't so bad to complain.' If this is going through your mind, this is showing empathy, which is good. To say this out loud to the customer is switching their response to your experience. This is not good. Don't! It is important to keep the conversation about them, not you.

The key is to describe yourself by using 'I' when talking to them to demonstrate what you have understood. Avoid using the word 'you' directly, as this can be perceived as attacking and making a judgement of them. For example, if you say, 'You are angry', the response is likely to be 'No, I'm not', or by saying 'You are frustrated', again the response is likely to be 'No, I'm not'. When using 'I', it is taking ownership of what you have understood about them from your perspective. This is something the customer cannot challenge. For example, when I say 'I'm get the impression that you are frustrated with your experience', this is me taking ownership of my truth. The other person cannot response with 'No, you are not getting that impression.' It's my truth.

Here are some phrases that might help you:
- What I understand is...
- It seems that...
- What I'm hearing is...
- I'm not sure I'm fully understanding, what I think I'm understanding is...
- I get the impression that...

Then add the specifics to the customer's situation.

You don't need to go over each and every point they have made. Here are a few examples, bearing in mind we don't have the body language and tone of voice to consider in these responses:

- The delivery person was rude to you.
- The soup is cold and bland.
- I get the impression that we've let you down.
- This is not what you expected.
- I'm sensing that you are frustrated, having been passed through various departments.

This is not agreeing or disagreeing, it's simply reflecting in a clear and succinct way what you have understood. It leaves the customer with the impression that you have understood them (you have). Many people don't feel heard or understood, and not feeling heard is at the nub of most emotion.

This is the best gift that you can give to your customer, to give them the sense that you have understood them. It is personalised and shows that you have paid attention to what they have said. It is the fundamental foundation that is required. Without it, the customer will have the impression that you are following a process that doesn't account for them, their feelings, emotions and perspective.

To re-iterate, as Stephen Covey says, 'Seek first to understand'. Listen and show that you have understood. Once this is done and clarified, the next steps can be taken.

Step 4: Respond

As soon as the customer has agreed that 'yes', this is exactly how they are feeling about their situation, you can then respond in a way that the customer senses that you truly care. It is important that the body language, tone of voice and words used are all expressing genuine care and interest in the customer.

Body language: Eye contact, with a calm and genuine caring look on your face. Body leaning slightly towards the customer to express interest. Feet separate and firmly on the floor. Body standing straight. (No leaning or crossed legs or feet.)

Tone of voice: Calm and clear. Slower and deeper tone than your normal.

Words: To be genuine and caring, such as 'I'm so sorry this has happened, this would not have been our intention. Thank you for sharing your experience with me. I really appreciate you taking the time to let me know.'

Often, I have heard service professionals say sorry with their head down and mumbling in the most insincere tone. They may as well not have said anything.

If you going to do this, do it well.
Get the customer back on your side.

It's so easy to do—be sincere and genuine. Remember your intention is to do a good job. Your team's aspiration is to ensure all customers leave your business thinking and feeling valued. Ideally, they will leave with what they wanted in the first place.

The customer may respond or may not. The next step is to strive to understand how you can resolve the situation to the customer's needs and expectations.

Step 5: Ask questions

You cannot possibly know what the ideal solution might be for the customer. This is why there is no point in considering possible solutions when the customer is talking through their complaint or judging them on what you believe they want. In my experience, so many service professionals go straight to offering money off, often thinking the person is a professional complainer and so they're just wanting to pay less. To some customers, money off is the biggest insult, it's really not about money for them. It's generally the principle that's it gone wrong or that their expectations have not been met that is the issue. It's not for us to assume that the customer's bank balance is similar to ours. The customer has agreed to pay the price that was quoted; hence they are in your business. They expected the product to be right, not faulty or delivered in a way they find unacceptable for that price.

We need to remember that every circumstance with customers based on their situation will give a different response based on what is happening in their life.

Continue your apology with:

'I'm wondering what I can do for you to take a step forward in resolving this situation?'

The question you ask needs to be appropriate to the circumstance. When I have been in a situation where the product or service can't be replaced as it's an experience (birthday party or weekend away, etc.), I've used the expression 'I wish I could turn the clocks back and demonstrate our ability to get this right. I'm wondering what I can do to restore your faith in us?' This is encouraging the customer to tell me so I can strive to meet their expectations.

This gives us a great opportunity to gather more information.

Of course, customers vary in what they expect. I wish I could give you a list of 'with this situation, do this', 'with that situation, do that' but that isn't possible. You know your business best and can gauge what kind of things are acceptable to ensure a win for the customer and a win for you and your business. It might be worth giving this some thought now, so you have some great ideas ahead of time.

In my experience, when you have reflected what you have understood to the customer, this is usually enough. The relief of you understanding the customer is the greatest compensation they could ask for. I've had so many customers who say, 'I don't want anything, I just wanted you to know so this won't happen again.' Or 'I'm glad that you're understanding.' Listening to understand and reflecting back your understanding really is magic!

Every single complaint we receive is unique, based on the circumstances of the customer, along with the circumstances in your team or business.

There might be times when you feel you are not authorised within your business to agree to what the customer has asked for. This is, as already mentioned, another reason for having an organisational policy in how you handle customer complaints and who has that authority. You might ask the customer for a moment whilst you check with your manager. This is so much better than getting the manager, for the customer to potentially share their story all over again. If the customer doesn't want to wait, offer an alternative solution so they can make the most of their time. This might be they do what they need to do— perhaps go shopping—or you call them back at a time that is suitable for them. If they are willing to wait, go to your line manager and gain their insight, explain the situation in brief and outline the expectation of the customer. Ask if you can meet the customer's expectation. You should gain a clear response from your line manager—yes or no. If no, agree alternative solutions with them that might match their expectations. The service professional then returns to the customer with the outcome of the conversation.

Some customers demand to speak to the manager, or there might be circumstances where you or your team feel ill-equipped to handle the customer's complaint. If getting the manager is the required action, it's important that the way this is done is not going to add to the customer's distress.

Let's put ourselves in the customer's shoes for a moment. We're annoyed, we've told the service professional, they respond with 'I'll get my manager'. They get the manager. The manager introduces themselves (well I hope they do!) Then says, 'How can I help you?' In my mind, the customer will be thinking 'Oh my goodness! Do I need to tell you the whole story again?' In some cases, the customer might get even more frustrated and shout and yell even more.

If you choose to get the manager, please ensure you share the key points of what the customer is complaining about and give your manager their name if you have it. It's then important that the manager approaches the customer with 'Good morning/afternoon/evening [NAME], I believe you're not happy with [detail the key points].' Allow the customer to respond with 'yes, that's right' or allow them to add to any key points they want to re-iterate. The manager can then apologise and start to explore suitable solutions.

In an exceptional experience, the service professional would have the confidence to know what they can and cannot agree to. This is impressive. What this communicates to the customer is that

this business is serious about service.

That no matter who I speak to, they are qualified to take ownership of the situation. EXCEPTIONAL!

In some circumstances, the customer may respond to your question of 'What can I do for you?' with, 'You tell me. What can you do?' This is when you need to offer a number of possible solutions to give the customer choice. Choice is important, not one solution and that's it. Here are some examples:

- Replace the item or a return visit to experience again.
- Offer an appropriate alternative product, maybe a more superior product.
- Replace and deliver.
- Fast track the order.
- Refund, discount, discount off next time, a voucher for future use.

There are many options. Let the customer make a choice that is right for them. Of course, this needs to be agreed beforehand to enable staff to have this power.

It's important that you are clear with your response and gain the customer's agreement to it.

Then you need to do it. Make what you've agreed happen. This needs to be timely, i.e. instant. Do it. This is creating the exceptional experience that leads to customer loyalty.

When you close the conversation with the customer, remain calm and genuine. Reiterate your appreciation for their feedback. Apologise again for the mistakes that have been made. Express your desire to see them again in the future.

When this happens, the customer often thanks you for your help. At times, they also apologise for having been rude to you earlier. This doesn't always happen. All I can say is have a go. Keep practising these steps and see what happens. Challenge yourself with new phrases that you feel comfortable with and use them in a way that is genuinely you.

To put this into perspective in everyday life, when I go into a coffee shop and order a coffee, the price is approximately £4. If the coffee served is not as expected and I express my dissatisfaction, when the service professional goes straight for 'I'm sorry, would you like your money back?' the answer is 'No'. I just want a coffee that I can consume. Bear in mind the varying circumstances of the customer and situation. Imagine if the service has been slow and I'm already short of time, the coffee is awful, and this is expressed to the service professional. The ideal solution might not be a replacement coffee, due to the lengthy service times. In this case, I might ask for my money back.

Ideally, no matter what my circumstances are, if the service professional states 'I'm sorry, we've clearly made a mess of your coffee. I'd like to ensure you leave happy today. What can I do for you to put this right?' I'd respond very easily with, 'I don't want another as I'm in a rush.' Having listened to my response, they could respond with 'How about we offer you two complimentary vouchers, one to replace today's and the second as an apology for today's coffee.' Then pass me the vouchers there and then. WOW! Of course, what they are doing is ensuring I return. I can get on with my day without being delayed any further. They have a second and third chance to demonstrate they can get their coffee right. Also, it demonstrates that they are confident that this situation was a 'one off' and not aligned to their aspirations as a coffee shop. Perfect. Placing me at the centre in how they respond.

Notes

Step 6: Make it memorable

The ultimate response is to make it memorable—in a good way. Follow up or add on something the customer didn't expect that makes them feel special and considered.

During the conversation you have with your customer you will know what would be a personalised follow up that is unique to them. This is why listening is so important. It gives you more information. This is when you have their heart and mind and your business is the obvious option when they need the services or product you sell.

Here's an example to bring the six steps up to now into reality:

CASE STUDY

Be there:
I was the manager on duty on this particular day when a call was put directly through to my extension. I was greeted by an irate customer who had a whole list of issues that he was not impressed with. At the time, it felt like he was never going to stop, going through the detail and repeating the same point over and over again. The pause arrived when he had finished with his emotion. I was about to speak in the pause when he filled the moment of silence with 'I'll put my wife on.' Oh, my goodness, she was worse than him. She didn't seem to draw a breath and she carried on and on like a runaway train. Sure enough, the pause arrived. She had said all that she wanted to say.

Watch the signals:
During their explanation, I could sense that they were hugely frustrated and felt let down from the many empty promises they had experienced from us.

Listen:
I remained silent throughout their explanation. I was totally focused on them. I reflected on one sentence: 'I get the impression that we've let you down.' Her response, which seemed to be in a relieved tone was 'You have'.

We both felt that sense of relief.

Respond:
I responded with 'I'm really sorry, this sounds awful. It would never be our intention for you to have experienced so many things to go wrong like this. I really would like to find a suitable solution that would work for you now. What would be best thing I can do to help?'

I listened some more. They knew exactly what they wanted. This issue in summary was they had arrived at the hotel earlier in the week and found their room to be uncomfortable due to the air-conditioning. They moved their room to find it was unsuitable. Our team had been delayed in assisting them. They were told that something would be done ready for when they returned to the hotel. Nothing had been done. This is when they called me. When I asked what I could do, they wanted to move to a room that met their requirements with the air-conditioning working effectively. It was late, it was not my place to suggest a change in room, especially when they had already moved and had been promised further action that hadn't taken place.

I made the arrangements to make what we agreed happen. There was no money mentioned or considered by either party. They asked for something that was relatively easily fixed.

I checked the following day with the team to see if the customer was happy. They were. We had made the correction in time to ensure the rest of their experience was memorable for positive reasons.

Make it memorable:
After checking with the team that these customers were happy, I wrote a note to them. In the note, I thanked them for sharing their feedback with me, and I apologised again for the inconvenience they had experienced. I enclosed my business card and invited them to contact me directly if there was anything else I might be able to assist with.

They texted me on their way home to thank me for my help and to say how they enjoyed their time once the issue had been resolved.

On reflection from this, consider:
- Had you been the client in this example, how would you be feeling?
- As the client, what would you have been thinking?

Before thinking about your business, here are a few of my thoughts:
- The customer knew exactly what they wanted.
- I remained genuinely focused and interested in understanding them and their situation.
- At no point during the time that I was listening to the customer did I allow my thoughts drift off into thinking of possible solutions or making any kind of judgement about them.
- I definitely did not judge them by my own perspective, i.e. I'd want my money back; they're paying a fortune for this. They knew the prices; they wouldn't have even considered our product if they weren't prepared to pay these rates.
- I know from my previous experiences that offering money off can be very insulting to many people. It's not all about the money. It's more about caring about them and giving them options to suit them. The best way to do this is ask or give them a selection of suitable solutions—that's if they ask you what can be done.
- I remained calm and focused throughout.
- The customer was grateful for my help and follow up. It felt good.

Thinking about your business:
- What do you and your team need in order to be confident to want to support all of your customers should they be in any way dissatisfied?
- What benefits would you see within your business if they did handle complaints in this way?

There are so many ways to make it memorable. Here are some I've used:

- Speak to the customer after the event when I next see them to make sure what we said would happen did happen and have a friendly chat with them so I get to know them even more.
- Write a note to the customer, thanking them for taking the time to share their feedback.
- Send flowers as an additional apology.
- Invite them back at a time that is aligned to their celebration. Give them a personalised note to greet them back. Possible add 'please call me directly if there is anything you need.'
- Send a voucher to use in the future for a return visit.

Most of these have little cost. The most important element is that it is thoughtful, considered and, most of all, personalised to them and their situation. Not many service professionals do this, it takes too much brain power. The easy option is to process customers like cookie cutters and then the customers don't feel valued at all.

Get your team together to consider how they might have dealt with previous complaints to make the solution memorable should they be able to turn the clocks back. This will help you and your team think 'personalised'.

It's also very important to ensure you relate to the previous experience when this customer comes back. Let them know that if anything is not quite as they'd expect to please let you know straight away. Then of course you do it. We need to treat these customers as VIP's, as they are VERY IMPORTANT PEOPLE. They are the lifeline to your business success. Remember, without them we have nothing.

Ideally, everyone in your organisation would have this mindset. If this was the case, all your teams would be equipped with the skills to address any kind of customer complaint, little whinge or concern. What would this do for your reputation? It would prove that you place the customer at the centre of all that you and your team do. Everyone would be interested and equipped to address the needs of all customers in the most efficient and effective way. Your team will soon realise the value they bring to the success of your business.

Notes

STAGE 4.
BE EXCEPTIONAL

Create and embed the *Zest for Life* method to constantly and consistently measure and improve your service delivery.

BE **EXCEPTIONAL**

N
ow you have all the ingredients to 'Be exceptional'. You have reviewed each of the basic sensory standards of see, hear, smell, taste and feel. From these, your customers make a first impression on whether they like or dislike what your business is about. Gaining the loyalty of each customer, one by one, to win their hearts and minds, is achieved by following the *6 Steps to Exceptional Service*. This will happen throughout your customers' experience with your business at the beginning, middle and end. Having these in place is setting you, your team and business up for success. However, it is important to remain open to making the experience even better, and to ensure your team is confident in handling any customers who are dissatisfied. If you believe having no complaints is something to celebrate, please review the statistics on page 166.

You now have the three key building blocks to create an exceptional experience for your customers:
1. Sensory Service Standards for all customers
2. 6 Steps to Exceptional Service for each individual customer
3. Confidence when dealing with feedback

This has been mentioned before and will be mentioned again before the end:

Exceptional Customer Service Makes Sense, Business Sense.

The challenge is that we all want exceptional results NOW! In reality, it takes time. If you take the time now to consider the ideal outcome you are striving for as you did in the Introduction and Chapter 1, you can then consider your first steps. It doesn't matter where you are now, it's about gradually upgrading over time. The aim is for you and everyone in your team to be clear about what good looks and feels like. Then you can start looking at what exceptional feels like.

There should not be one day that goes by when your service levels are ignored. If it is, this could be the beginning of the end for your reputation. If the service your customers experience is not central to all you do, your loyal customers will eventually notice what your competitors do. I hope you don't sit back and watch this happen to your business, as it won't be long until you have little business at all.

It's SO important that everyone in the business is clear about what good service looks and feels like. This then enables them to deliver. The idea is that everyone within your team become 'Service Inspectors'. A little like the 'Hotel Inspector', they can see the service through the customers' eyes, so they don't become complacent about their behaviour and the state of the business environment. The clearer people are the better. When people are confident about what they need to do and why they need to do it, there are no squabbles. Clarity is crucial. Measurement is vital.

What gets measured get done.

Notes

Here's an example of when this approach worked.

Whilst working in a busy successful hotel, where my manager's style of leadership was 'managing by walking about', he would often ask us what we saw as we walked into the entrance of the hotel. As a result of previous conversations we'd had, we would know what he'd expect. We would have already checked the windows and glass doors, ensuring they were free from fingerprints and smears. The plants in the flowerpots looked fresh and healthy. He'd guide us to take a closer look, moving the hanging flowers which cascaded over the large ornate planters to reveal cigarette packets that had been left by customers. We never needed telling twice about that same issue, our pride wouldn't allow it!

During my performance review discussion, he asked how things were going. It was obvious that things weren't as good as they could have been. In our morning meetings, there seemed to be more complaints than normal. As a result of my review, part of my role changed to have informal conversations with customers in the morning to see how their stay was going or had been. If they responded with "It was alright", I'd probe a little further. I'd ask if there was one thing that could have improved, what it would be. The customers knew the answer to that question and gave us some great insight into what we could improve. The whole team was keen to learn from the customers and right any wrongs. I would write to the customer to thank them for their feedback and share with them a brief outline of who I'd shared their comments with and what we had done, with a message of looking forward to welcoming them back to the hotel in the future. What was amazing about this was that I had letters back from the customers, thanking me for my thank you letter! Here's where the measurement comes in. A graph was created, presenting the type of comments we'd had and whether they were product or service related. This was placed in the staff restaurant for the hotel team to see. Over a three-month period, the complaints reduced.

Numbers are helpful to gauge the effectiveness of the procedures that have been put in place. When there is measurement, it is possible to adjust behaviours and tasks to influence the results and keep on a positive track. They also give an opportunity to celebrate. It creates confidence and a huge feel-good factor.

This is just like the example shared in the 'Feel' chapter relating to Manchester United winning the league. Everyone inside and outside of the team kept a close eye on the numbers after each match, which accumulate across the football season. For any sporting game, the scoreboard is super important as it is monitored by everyone because we all want to know who is winning or losing. This creates focus for the team playing, as this informs them which action needs to be taken to influence the scoreboard positively.

There is one thing that is challenging about measuring service and that is the discipline to maintain and monitor the results. If you think about sales, in most organisations there's a whole accounting team employed to gather financial data, give feedback and monitor the revenue. Measuring service should be everyone's job, making this a natural part of everyone's job description to identify and deliver exceptional service, react and measure. If it is done well, senior management would take an interest, make note of the figures and act accordingly.

As a first step, you might want to take a snapshot of the whole of your business, so you can assess the before and after. To be fair to you and your team, I would do this privately, so it is realistic and not an opportunity to point out the error of everyone's ways. It's like the before and after photos people take of themselves before and after their health kick. Its real purpose is for you to share the feel-good factor when the team is making positive progress. Ideally this would be in twelve months' time when the *Service Standards Checklists* have been embedded into your team's daily routine.

If you choose to carry out a full assessment, the complete set of service standards is listed in Appendix A. Alternatively you can download these from *Zest for Life*'s website. You might want to ensure these standards are suitable for your industry or business. Make alterations to ensure they work for you whilst maintaining the essence of service expectations. There is no point in cutting corners as your customers will soon notice. The more challenging the standards you create, the greater pride this will instil in your team—and you, of course.

Remember, the wording of the standards is to state the standard required that will lead to 'Yes', giving you a positive point. Otherwise, you may become confused by focusing on what you don't want. These service standards are to be observable, so you can assess objectively whether they are applied or not.

As already stated, complete the whole audit now and again in twelve months' time, then make this part of an annual routine. This will keep your service at exceptional levels, help you maintain all the basic standards, and encourage you to make the appropriate upgrades as your business develops and customers' expectations grow.

In some organisations, they engage an external auditor to assess service standards and to gain an objective view of their service. There are some who prepare for that pending visit and even ensure that the inspector receives the VIP treatment. This is crazy! I appreciate you want a great result, however if that person gets different treatment from the actual paying customers, the process is not giving you the objective data you need.

The full audit is optional and you may choose to go straight into just using the 10 service standards to gain momentum and a sense of achievement, rather than tackling the whole thing initially.

If you have carried out the exercises throughout the book so far, you will already have an idea of the 10 service standards that you have selected to observe within your business, which will make the overall bigger picture doable. You will have 10 bite-size chunks of service standards that are easy to influence and master and will build confidence and team engagement. The process, when embedded within your organisation, will encourage your team members to understand their own contribution and feel valued as they see the positive impact of their actions. After all, we all enjoy feeling part of a successful team.

Here's how to make your service count. If you want this badly enough, the next 10 steps will soon be a way of life if you want to be exceptional.

There is no room for complacency.

1. Complete a full audit (optional)

As mentioned earlier in this chapter, if you want to gain an overall summary of your service delivery standards right now, then carry out a full audit against all the service standards. This will give you a start point measure. These are outlined in Appendix A or you can download them from the *Zest for Life* website. Ideally, these results would be kept private and not shared with your team. You don't want your team to potentially feel deflated before implementing the *10-Service Standards Checklists*. Consider sharing the results when the second audit is completed in twelve months' time, to show them the before and after, which will be far more motivating for them. It's so much better for your team to start on a positive note, where the improvement seems doable.

Adapt the standards so they work for your business. As already mentioned, when wording the standards, make sure that they outline the required standards to give you a 'yes' outcome. This will mean that every positive service standard will create an additional score.

As you carry out the audit, capture notes of what you see, so you have an idea of where you and your team are performing well or where additional support might be required.

Carry out the complete audit of service standards and keep the result somewhere safe, so you can compare when you complete your next full audit.

2. Initial Service Standards Checklist

If you have completed the activity after each of the sensory chapters of see, hear, smell, taste and feel, you will already have the first *Service Standards Checklist* ready to start using.

If you haven't completed this exercise as you read through the book, now is the time to select the service standards that you'd like to influence and embed within your business. Select the two service standards from the end of each chapter of see, hear, smell, and taste, and one from each of the 'feel' chapters. Flex these where necessary to meet the needs of your business, i.e. if you don't serve any food or drinks as part of your offering, you can skip this and replace them with two standards from the other senses. Overall, the aim is for you to have 10 service standards. The blank template is found in Appendix B.

3. Think like an inspector

To make it super clear, the wording of each of your standards needs to outline what you are looking for, so when this is observed you give yourself a positive score. This will give you a true reflection of adherence to the standards. For example, if you write something like 'Do you see dust on work surfaces and shelves?' If there is dust, this will lead to the person carrying out the observation responding with a 'yes'. This will then skew your score as you will have a higher score for a dusty surface! This should read, 'Are all work surfaces and shelves free from dust?' The more positive responses the better. It will also ensure that you and your team know what you want your customers to experience, rather than negative standards of what you don't want.

Have a go at using *10-point Service Standards Checklists*. Read the standard. If you stand in your business, will you observe x, y and z? If you are assessing telephone service standards, what will you notice or hear?

The most important aspect of this is to ensure you capture what you actually notice. It either did or did not happen. There is no point in making excuses for everyone such as 'Oh I know they normally do this; I'll give this a point or tick.' This is not helping you and your team to become exceptional. Remember, consistently high standards are to be delivered to every customer.

There are some samples in Appendix C to give you an idea of how your *10-point Service Standards Checklists* might look. It's best for you to create your own and get others in the team involved if possible, which leads us on to the next point.

4. Get others involved

When you have your *10-point Service Standards Checklist*, share these with one trusted colleague within your team. Gain their thoughts about the standards. Explain to them what you are striving to achieve, the reasons why, and how you plan to introduce the *Service Standards Checklist.*

Listen to their thoughts and make any appropriate alterations according to their recommendations. Ensure they are aligned to your desired outcome and make sure you're not taken off the point, or persuaded to accept average service standards.

Discuss any recommendations which are unclear so that you come up with a well-defined *Service Standards Checklist* that can be observed. I find that sometimes people will state things like 'I think we need to see teamwork.' My question is 'How do you observe this?' If this is something that you want to promote, then what will be observed would be: 'See good collaboration between the team', or 'Hear good comments within the team about each other', or 'See positive body language between the team.' For each observation, there is space to note what you did see, so the checklist can be reviewed objectively. This will help you and your team know the behaviours that are helpful versus those that are not.

Ask this trusted colleague to share the *Service Standards Checklists* with their team. Gain their insight. Allow them to practise by carrying out observations against the checklists on themselves. Gather their reactions and ask how they have got on. What have they noticed that is going well? What do they believe they can do to be even better?

Allow a couple of weeks for the teams to get used to the *Service Standards Checklists*. Encourage all team members to complete a checklist. Have one checklist completed each day, by a different colleague at different times of the day.

Even if you are completing this process to measure your own personal levels of service, you could still ask others to give their opinion. More on this in the next point.

5. Once a week or daily

Each checklist will take approximately 5-10 minutes to complete, once a week or even daily if you and your team are keen to embed the standards. The *Service Standards Checklist* is to be used for all aspects of your business. Wherever your team is working, a checklist can be used. If you want to adapt different checklists for specific areas, then do so. These need to be relevant.

There are different ways you can approach this, to suit you and your team:

A. You want to take ownership of your own service delivery.

B. You want to encourage your team to take ownership of their service delivery.

C. You want to encourage the whole organisation to take ownership of their service delivery.

As I've mentioned previously, ideally it should be part of everyone's job description, but this is not always possible. Whichever approach you choose, these steps apply. The only exception is that if you are assessing yourself, in which case you (of course) will not require to gain the team buy-in. Generally speaking, we are the biggest critic of ourselves. However, there are some people whose ego leads them to believe they are magnificent in all they do. If this is the case, and you suspect you are like this or have characters like this in your team, it is even more important to notice how the customers respond to the service that is offered. Be honest and objective. This might be tricky for some colleagues with big egos to accept. Remind your team that getting the perspective of others is so important. Everyone will soon get on track. This will give you space to grow, develop and be exceptional.

Here are three options for how you could complete the checklists:

Option A: If you are committed to ensuring that, as an individual, you are delivering exceptional service, assess yourself on a daily basis. Imagine viewing the service you have delivered to your customers from a 'bird's eye' perspective, as though you are viewing your interactions as a third person. Be honest with yourself and what you noticed. Complete your own *Service Standards Checklist*; you're likely to be harsher on yourself than others would. You might like to ask a colleague to assess you and gain their perspective. The more perspectives you can have the better.

Option B: If you are wanting to carry out the *Service Standards Checklist* with your direct team, devise a schedule. Ask who will carry out the checklist at what time. Ideally, you'd spread the timing over different times of the day to ensure the whole of the shift or day is assessed against the same standards consistently. Make sure that you personally carry out a checklist as part of this schedule, so you can see for yourself what is happening.

Option C: Issue one *Service Standards Checklist* for each department or area within your business, for one person in each area to carry out a checklist on another area of the business. For example, person A from Department A will check Department B, Person B from Department B will check Department C, etc., so there is an objective view. Encourage all leaders to get involved and carry out checklists, so that they remain in the real world and keep their feet firmly on the shop floor, knowing exactly what your customers are experiencing. Give the people who are carrying out the checklists one day to complete them, then ask them to share the completed checklist with the team they've just watched. This encourages them to feel valued and involved—this is not the secret service! Return the completed *Service Standards Checklist* to one central person who will collect the data; the 'Service Accountants'. This person will then share the results with the relevant department, so they can learn from what was observed with the intention of getting even better. You might want each department to share their results at a team meeting or briefing. Ideally, they'd highlight what they have learned and what they intend to do to increase their scores. There should be an open approach, so everyone feels treated fairly and encouraged by the progress.

No matter which option you choose, each person is to carry out the checklist ideally at a time when customers are present. If customers aren't present, notice the surroundings as this is very much part of the checklist if you have selected items from the sensory standards. Carry out the checklist, allow about 10 minutes to ensure there is an opportunity to see the standards in action. A simple yes or no for each of the ten standards. Also note down what is witnessed for each point. For example, you might have 'Did the team member greet your customer as soon as they arrived into their department?' Did you see this, yes or no? If yes, note down what exactly you saw. Perhaps 'As soon as the customer arrived, the colleague looked at the customer, smiled and said, 'Good morning.' Or no, 'No customer arrived at the time of observation.'

This whole process is aimed to be supportive and encouraging rather than critical and demeaning. If this moves to have a sense of policing, the spirit of the service you and your team offer will be less genuine and less likely to have the desired outcome.

If colleagues need some help, this would be done privately with guidance and support, so that they have the opportunity to gain clarification and improve.

Allow time for this process to be embedded and for the team to feel confident about what they are doing. This could take up to three months.

6. Create a scoreboard

Once you and the team are clear and confident about the standards, it's time to publish the scores internally, so that the whole team can see how the organisation is progressing. This is to create energy and focus on how well you are doing, just like a sporting scoreboard. Are we winning or losing? Everyone knows what needs to be done to win. Ask questions such as: How can we have a whole team approach to winning? What support or guidance might be needed for some players/colleagues within our team?

If you are assessing yourself, do the same thing. You might want to do this in the back of a notebook so you can see the progress that you are making.

7. Celebrate success

The huge benefit is there is a feel-good factor when the team scores a 10. It creates that 'YES' moment with you and your team. What is even better is when a 10 is scored consistently. There's a feeling of confidence and focus within the team. However, they will soon realise that if they become complacent the scores will drop.

Be clear about what success is. Remember what you set out to do. Success would be an average score of 9 or 10 for the whole team or organisation. This will encourage team collaboration and support. The mindset is that if one team is struggling, the whole of the organisation will not succeed. If one team seems to have mastered high scores, encourage them to share how they have achieved this.

Reputation is everything.

How you celebrate success is entirely up to you. In my experience, a personal 'thank you' related to the standards makes a big impact. High fives and team recognition is also effective.

When you are assessing yourself, this brings credibility to what you are doing. Other people might remark on the improvements that you have made, whether they are customers or your colleagues. Most of all, you will notice. This will support you in knowing that you are doing a good job and is likely to assist you throughout your career.

People who deliver exceptional service get noticed.

8. Learn and take steps to be exceptional

When your team is consistently achieving 9's and 10's, review your notes from steps 2, 3, and 4 then consider updating the *Service Standards Checklists* to upgrade your customers' service experience. You could use the second *Service Standards Checklist* from the *6 Steps to Exceptional Service* chapter. Get your team involved to maintain their interest and motivate them to take the service standards to the next level. Consider making some alterations from their feedback, whilst remaining true to the overall ambition.

9. Renew, embed, upgrade, repeat

Continue with the new standards for the next 3-6 months, until the team reach their consistent 9's and 10's across all departments. Then repeat.

These steps will upgrade your service to exceptional levels. Over time you will have confidence that service is central to what your team does. When you have new colleagues who join your team, you will find that the team will share these *Service Standards Checklists*. Help and guide the team so they know exactly what good looks like. Make this a part of how you work each and every day, so everyone is confident that service is measured.

10. Complete an audit (optional)

On the anniversary of your initial overall audit, you may want to carry out a second one to compare the before and after. The outcome will be positive when the process has been introduced with consideration, guidance and positive energy.

This can be part of your annual assessment, so you have that holistic view at least once a year. You may want to upgrade the service standards once your team have grasped this level of exceptional. By now, your customers and teams will have some great ideas about upgrading the service beyond the current standards.

Here's a flow chart that might assist you with your implementation. Appendix C also contains a sample *Service Standards Checklist* for phone use.

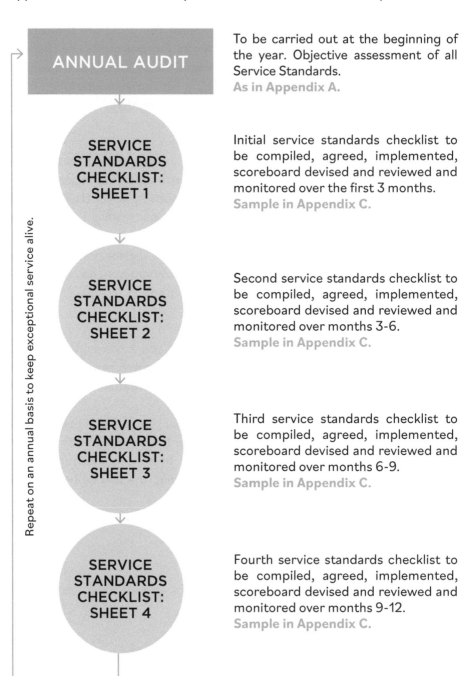

ANNUAL AUDIT

To be carried out at the beginning of the year. Objective assessment of all Service Standards.
As in Appendix A.

SERVICE STANDARDS CHECKLIST: SHEET 1

Initial service standards checklist to be compiled, agreed, implemented, scoreboard devised and reviewed and monitored over the first 3 months.
Sample in Appendix C.

SERVICE STANDARDS CHECKLIST: SHEET 2

Second service standards checklist to be compiled, agreed, implemented, scoreboard devised and reviewed and monitored over months 3-6.
Sample in Appendix C.

SERVICE STANDARDS CHECKLIST: SHEET 3

Third service standards checklist to be compiled, agreed, implemented, scoreboard devised and reviewed and monitored over months 6-9.
Sample in Appendix C.

SERVICE STANDARDS CHECKLIST: SHEET 4

Fourth service standards checklist to be compiled, agreed, implemented, scoreboard devised and reviewed and monitored over months 9-12.
Sample in Appendix C.

Repeat on an annual basis to keep exceptional service alive.

With regards to making the customer experience 'memorable', you might want to collect what it is the team do that have positive impacts on the customers. Share these with the rest of the team so these 'one off' experiences become the norm for you, your team and your business. This is what makes you stand apart from your competitors.

This will give you and your team confidence that your service is at a level you want. Your customers will continue to write reviews from their perspective, from which you and your team will continue to learn. However, rather than potentially getting frustrated with any subjective comments, you will now have the confidence that your team is focusing on what is important for your business at each moment in time. It is important to embrace all feedback, learn and improve.

It won't take long for you to see the difference.

Here's a little story of how soon this approach made a positive impact in a hotel when this process was applied.

The hotel was mid-way through a ground floor refurbishment. The old layout had a dedicated bar and lounge, with a coffee stand close to the hotel entrance. The team who manned the coffee stand would wait diligently behind the counter. Offering table service was not part of their service. The bar and lounge were combined with the coffee stand in the new layout and the two teams were joined together as one. The coffee stand team were loyal, long-serving colleagues who liked their old style of service.

A few weeks ahead of the new ground floor unveiling, we carried out training to share the new approach to service to include table service. The team was ready as the new look was opened. On day one I took the Service Standards Checklist to capture what I noticed. This was completed alongside the person who was on duty. We checked the standards together.

By the time day three arrived, they were completing the Service Standards Checklist themselves. In the second week, they were completing the checklist, making the appropriate adjustments, e.g. ordering new menus to ensure they had sufficient stock that met the required immaculate standards we had agreed. The team offered table service and were pro-active about looking after the customers, rather than standing and waiting for coffee orders. The transformation was outstanding in such a short period of time. The team seemed to adjust their ways as a result of the manner in which we had introduced the change. Overall, the main objective was to improve the service. They continued to be passionate about the service they delivered. The team received many compliments and the hotel was hugely successful.

Get started with your first 10 service standards. Make sure your team is involved and fully understand what you are striving to achieve and why. Value their thoughts and contributions and see how soon the standards are embraced, embedded and improved.

Notes

Notes

LEADING

You have picked up this book because you want to be the best you can be in your work and you are passionate about making a difference to the customer experience in your business. You may have picked it up because you have an ambition to one day lead a team or may have picked it up because you are already a leader and want to improve the standards in your team. If you are not yet a team leader, you could 'manage upwards' and suggest some changes when you next speak to your manager. Explain the benefits. The reputation of you, your team and your business will be enhanced if you adopt all aspects of what you have learned.

To re-emphasise, you can adopt all aspects of the 'Be exceptional' chapter. Create your own *10-point Service Standards Checklist* and assess yourself against them. Develop your own scoreboard and self-assess over time. As soon as you are achieving 9's and 10's, upgrade your *10-point Service Standards Checklists* to exceptional levels. Over time, your own personal reputation will shine.

If you are leading a team and want them to embrace the changes you want for your customers, with the ambition to reap the financial benefits, you will need the drive to keep the process alive. It requires you to be as focussed as any finance person is about collecting data about the revenue that is generated in your business.

*Make looking after your customers the
most important thing your team does.*

Everyone in your team has to prioritise customers over tasks. By placing the customer at the heart of everything you do, your customer will sense the generous spirit of service and will come back time and again. They will speak highly of you and will encourage others to visit too.

Every single person within your team is there for the customer. This includes the people behind the scenes. The 'Heart of House' team (as we call these team members in the hospitality world) have an impact on the customer. Remember, the mindset is that even if you're not serving a customer directly, then you are serving a colleague who is.

Here's an example of when this happened, which is in retail. A colleague had received a request from a customer for a product they knew was available in the stockroom, and all stock had sold from the shop floor. The colleague offered to get one for the customer. The colleague was in the stockroom searching for the item. The storeman noticed the shop floor colleague, asked her what she was looking for. He said he'd get her one and bring it to her on the shop floor. She was relieved. She returned to the customer, chatted and was friendly. The product arrived shortly after. The storeman was greeted by a very appreciative customer and colleague. The customer left happy, very pleased with the way they had been treated and saying that they look forward to seeing the shop floor colleague again soon.

Just a little focus on the purpose of your business goes a long way to help all people within the organisation.

Inspiring your team is important. Without your team, service delivery is impossible. In order for everyone in your business to be exceptional in all they do, they need clear direction. They need to feel motivated, believe that they perform well, have a leader who inspires them, a leader who is present, visible, communicates effectively, supports and guides them, and adopts a healthy and safe culture where everyone within it can flourish and grow.

If you'd like to explore how to do this, perhaps our *Exceptional Leadership Makes Sense* programme might assist. *Zest for Life* offers Leadership and Service workshops to train leaders in inspiring teams to be exceptional in all they do. If you're interested, please take a look at our website for more information - **www.zflltd.com**.

Notes

ENJOY EVERY
MOMENT

t has been a pleasure to share my passion for service, or more importantly, people. When we consider the needs of others, truly listening and delivering on expectations and more, everyone wins.

It sounds easy. However, it may not seem too easy—initially.

The key is to start at the beginning, and to be honest and true to yourself. Build your customer experience with the all-important foundational senses. Master these then slowly embed the next stage. It takes time. However, enjoy the steps as you take them, knowing that each step is a step closer to becoming exceptional. Celebrate getting the detail right, then move on.

I would love to know how you get on. Share your stories of success on:

Linkedin - ZFL (UK) Ltd or Sally Prescott, Warrington
Twitter - @ZFLltd,
Facebook – ZestforLifeLtd
Instagram - sally.prescott.52
Or send a message to us on our website **www.zflltd.com**

I would also love to know what you think of the book and the process so please take a few moments to post a review on whichever platform you bought this book.

You will also find blogs and more information about the services that we offer on the website, as well as an opportunity to register for our quarterly newsletter which is full of topical perspectives on how teams impact on customers and each other.

Keep focused, take it one step at a time and remember 'Exceptional Service Makes Sense, Business Sense.'

Have fun,

Sally ✳

ACKNOWLEDGEMENTS

Thank you to many fabulous clients, colleagues and friends who have encouraged me in anticipation of this long-awaited book. It has spurred me on to keep going, with the intention of making it exceptional, doable and to make a positive difference.

Thank you for all the fabulous businesses out there who deliver exceptional service, enabling me to use you as great live examples. I'm hoping these stories will inspire many others to follow your lead.

A personal thank you to my gorgeous husband, Jack, who has allowed me to get on with it, giving me the time and space to write. Thank you also for helping me to gain clarity when my thoughts may have been slightly cloudy. I love you, Jack.

A huge thank you to Siân-Elin Flint-Freel, my book mentor and editor, for her expertise, patience and guidance. Siân-Elin has made this book my reality. Having attended an event where she presented, I realised now is the time, after 10 years of pondering, to bring my first book idea to life. We mapped out the schedule for the book, then each month met via Zoom to review the writing and plan the next chapter or phase. I really would not have been able to do this without Siân. She is amazing and has a fabulous sense of humour. Thank you SO much, Siân, for being you and all your support.

ABOUT THE
AUTHOR

Sally Prescott is the director of Zest for Life, a learning and development company which supports teams across the UK who are committed to exceptional service and leadership and the benefits it brings to their business. She would love the UK to be a place where people enjoy their work, the people they work with and take pride in all they do.

She works with diverse clients such as: The Dorchester, The Dorchester Collection Academy, The Savoy, St. Ermin's, The Royal Horseguards, The Tower, The Grosvenor, Jumeirah, L'oscar, Amba Charing Cross, Figleaves, RBS, Bents Garden and Home, Thorpes Joinery, The Hari, London Grace, Royal Garden Hotel, Shangri-La, Sofitel, Ed's Easy Diner, and Aspen Healthcare.

She is licensed facilitator of Franklin Covey programmes 'The 7 Habits of Highly Effective People', 'Great Leaders, Great Teams, Great Results' and a ICF qualified and an accredited coach.

Sally is also a Trustee and the International Head of Training for Radio Lollipop, which is a charity whose volunteers provide care, comfort, play and entertainment for sick children in hospital. For 30 years, Sally has volunteered, recruited, trained, presented, organised conferences and helped the charity reach more sick children across the world.

APPENDIX **A**

Here are all the standards that are mentioned in the book. You could use them to complete your annual overall service standards audit. You may want to adapt or re-word these so that they are applicable to your business.

See Exceptional

Website and Social Media:

1. Are you proud of your website?

2. Is your website a true representative of your business?

3. Is it easy for your customers to make contact with you?

4. Would you want to buy from your business?

Outside your business:

5. When your customers arrive at your business, do they see gleaming, clean windows with no dust, streaks, smears, handprints or water marks on them?

6. When your customers arrive at your business, do they see attractive displays, a clean environment, healthy plants, etc.? Is it free from weeds and debris?

7. Is the door opened for customers?

8. Is the door clean? Free from fingerprints?

9. Are all areas in working order? Are all lamps working?

10. Do they see high hygiene scores where applicable?

Inside and throughout your business:

11. Do your customers see a colleague who is focused on them and offering an instant, warm and genuine welcome?

12. Do your customers see positive staff interactions between each other?

13. Do your customers see colleagues giving instant warm eye contact, standing straight and showing caring body language towards them?

14. Are your team well presented, looking smart and aligned to the company image?

15. Do you and your customer see all colleagues moving around the business

at an appropriate pace that looks calm and confident? i.e. not rushed or over relaxed

16. Do your customers see immaculate seating? Table tops, bases and seats free from dust, crumbs and debris?

17. Do your customers see soft furnishings plumped up as though no-one else has been there?

18. Do your customers see freshly vacuumed, swept or mopped flooring? That is free from debris, dust, dirt or grease?

19. Do your customers see clean vents and air filters that are free from dust and dirt? That are in a fully effective working order?

20. Do your customers see all literature immaculately presented, that is neat and tidy? Free from graffiti, rips and creases?

21. Do your customers see a well-maintained area? Free from scuffs on the paintwork? Are all lamps and lights in working order?

22. Do your customers see the information they want and need on immaculate materials? That is free from creases, debris, graffiti, rips?

23. Do your customers see positive interactions with other customers? Are all colleagues being helpful to all customers?

24. Do your customers see all colleagues giving their undivided attention to the customer they are interacting with? Listening careful and responding appropriately?

25. Do your customers see all colleagues prioritising the customer before tasks and their colleagues?

26. Do your customers see all decorations in your business that are clean, sparkling, fresh and well maintained? Do they see decorations that are aligned to the season?

27. Do your customers see all crockery immaculate? Free from cracks, chips and stains?

28. Do your customers see immaculate cutlery? Free from debris, water stains and smears?

29. Do your customers see healthy plants and flowers?

30. Do your customers see helpful notices which are well placed? Or do colleagues guide the customer in person to the correct place?

31. Do your customers see clean and inviting toilet facilities? That are sparkling clean and free from stains and excessive water around the sinks?

32. Do your customers see in cupboards, behind curtains, under beds or furniture, in walkways that are clean, free from clutter and debris?

Hear exceptional:

Website:

33. Do your customers hear clear, easily understood and positive messages from your website?

34. What music or audio do your customers experience on your website? Is it a good quality? Is it clear and free from tinny sounds?

35. What messages do your customers hear from online reviews by your customers? Do they gain a positive impression of your business?

Outside your business:

36. What do your customers hear as they arrive into your business? Is this aligned to the overall experience you would like them to have?

Inside and throughout your business:

37. Do your customers hear a genuine warm welcome for themselves and to all other customers?

38. Do your customers hear positive language with each and every interaction they have with a colleague?

39. Do your customers hear music that is complementary to the overall style and mood of your business?

40. Do your customers hear positive background noise, free from unwanted banging doors, clattering of operational activity not wanted to be heard by the customer? Free from maintenance or engineering noise?

41. Do your customers hear other customers complimenting the team and your business?

42. Do you and your colleagues sound confident, clear, concise and informative?

43. Do you and your colleagues respond with information that is aligned to your customers' needs?

44. Do you and your colleagues explain relevant information to your customers so they are fully informed? Rather than leaving them to potentially be caught out by the sign they didn't notice or the small print they haven't read? To be exceptional, you'd offer both.

45. Do your customers hear your colleagues engaging in friendly and appropriate conversation with them and other customers?

46. Do your customers hear your colleagues explore solutions to their needs?

47. Do your customers hear what the colleague has understood from their expectations?

48. Do your customers hear all colleagues greeting or acknowledging them throughout the business?

49. Do your customers hear full sentences that make sense?

50. Do your customers hear clear and succinct information they need to be aware of, in a way they understand?

51. Do you and your team have an agreed greeting when you answer the phone that showcases your business as you'd like?

52. Do your customers' calls get answered within your standard timescales?

53. Do your customers speak to your colleagues on the phone with no annoying background noises that may distract them from the conversation?

54. Do you and your colleagues give all customers on the phone your undivided attention? Focusing only on the caller?

55. Are all messages that are taken from your customers responded to as you'd like?

Smell exceptional:

Fresh people:

56. Do you and your team have fresh breath?

57. Do you and your team have fresh, clean body and hair? Free from nicotine, drugs or stale food or body odour?

58. Do you and your team's clothes smell fresh? Free from nicotine, drugs or stale food or body odour?

59. Do you and your team wear subtle and understated deodorants, perfume or aftershave which is not overpowering?

Fresh premises:

60. Are your premises fresh and thoroughly aired?

61. Are your premises free from the smell of overpowering cleaning products, bleach, etc.?

62. Are your plants and flowers smelling fresh and healthy? Do the flowers have fresh water?

63. Do you have delightful aromas that entice your customers to buy your products? Such as fresh bread, coffee, relaxing spa scents.

64. Are your toilets facilities aired?

65. Are your toilets free from overpowering cleaning product odours?

66. Are all your extractors fans clean and working effectively?

67. Are your premises free from poor maintenance odours?

68. Are your premises free from any musty, mould or stale food smells?

69. Are you premises promoting positive food aromas at the appropriate time of the day? e.g. fresh bread, fresh coffee, etc.

70. Are you premises free from the smell of stale fat or grease?

71. Are you using aromas to enhance your customer experience?

Taste exceptional:

Website:

72. Would what your customers see on your website appeal to your ideal customer's taste?

73. Does the food you sell look tasty?

74. Do the drinks look appetising?

Outside your business:

75. Is the style of your business meeting the needs and expectations of your ideal customers? Would the design meet their personal taste? Would it entice them into your premises?

76. Does your business have a clear style or theme that is recognisable to your ideal customer?

Inside and throughout your business:

77. Does the environment within your business complement the style and theme that is shown outside?

78. Does your business have a clear image that suits your business location. Is it:
    - Traditional?
    - Rustic?
    - Trendy?
    - Retro?
    - Gothic?
    - Light?
    - Bright?
    - Dark?
    - Dull?
    - Minimalistic?
    - Ornate?
    - Of course...add your own as this list could go on forever.

79. Does the food you sell or serve work well with the theme or style of business?

80. Do the drinks you sell or serve work well with the theme or style of business?

81. Is the food and drink you offer aligned to the tastes of your customers and not the person who buys or produces the products within your business?

82. Are all your food and drink items selling? Do you need to reconsider the items which are not selling?

83. Is the food and drink safe for your customers to eat? Is there good stock rotation?

84. Do you have a high food and drink hygiene score that you are proud of?

85. Is the hot food and drink you sell hot?

86. Is the cold food and drink you sell cold?

87. Is the hot food and drink you serve presented on a hot plate, warmed teapot and warm cup, mug or glass?

88. Is the cold food and drink you serve presented on a cold plate, chilled glass?

89. Does the food taste delicious? Can you identify the flavours?

90. Are the drinks amazing? Can you identify the flavours?

91. Is the food and drink served consistently fresh and tasting good?

Feel exceptional:

92. Are all areas where your customers sit or stand free from drafts?

93. Do your customers feel clean, polished surfaces?

94. Do your customers feel clean, polished surfaces underfoot?

95. Do your customers feel clean and freshly vacuumed flooring?

96. Do your customers feel quality products aligned to your business style?

97. Do your customers feel dry (where required—this wouldn't work in a swimming pool or spa!) surfaces throughout your business?

98. Do you feel positive vibes coming from your colleagues? Do they seem calm, confident and happy in their role?

99. Do you feel positive vibes when your colleagues interact with each other?

100. Do you feel positive vibes coming from your customers? If not, what action needs to be taken? Do your team know what to do about this kind of situations?

101. Do your customers feel the temperature is at the right level for their comfort?

102. Do your customers feel the atmosphere is clean and fresh? Not humid, damp or stale.

103. Do you and your team greet and acknowledge your customer as soon as they arrive into your business or premises?

104. Do you and your team greet and acknowledge your customers as they move around in your business or premises?

105. Do you and your team seem to genuinely want to look after your customers?

106. Do you and your team seem to genuinely care about your customers?

107. Do you and your team ask if they can assist your customers further at appropriate times for your customer?

108. Do you and your team make eye contact with your customers?

109. Do you and your team display open and welcoming body language that gives the customer the impression that you care?

110. Do you and your team communicate with your customers in a caring tone of voice?

111. Do you and your team communicate calmly and with confidence with your customers?

112. Do you and your team consider ways of making a customers' experience memorable? Such as a note of thanks to them, a note wishing them a happy birthday or anniversary, finding something out about them and offering assistance with this.

113. Do you and your team genuinely ask how your customer's experience was? With the intention of learning from that customer experience and gaining information to potentially improve for the future.

114. Do you and your team offer a genuine 'farewell' to your customers? With a message along the lines of 'We look forward to seeing you again'.

6 Steps to Exceptional Service

Be there

Consider these throughout your customer experience:

115. Are you and your team physically there/present to greet and acknowledge each and every customer?

116. Are you and your team mentally there/present to observe, fully engage to consider what your customers may want or need throughout?

117. Are you and your team looking up in anticipation for customers arriving into your business or your area of the business?

118. Do you or your team notice the arrival of a customer and open the door to your premises as they arrive?

119. Are you and your team ready to accept payment when the customer is ready?

120. Are you and your team present as the customer needs additional assistance?

121. Is there always one of your team present whilst a customer is present?

122. Do you and your team acknowledge each and every customer in a positive manner that indicates that you are there for them? i.e. a smile, a nod of the head, a good morning.

123. Do you and your team answer the phone within 3 rings?

124. Are you and your team attentive and focused only on the customer whilst on the phone?

Watch the signals

Consider these throughout your customer experience:

125. Do you and your team switch body language and tone to meet the needs of the customer? i.e. When the customer is looking happy, you welcome them positively. If they look concerned or serious, you welcome them with a calm tone.

126. Do you and your team offer assistance where it is clear the customer is needing additional help? i.e. notice their body language.

127. Do your customers receive instant assistance? i.e. within 3 seconds.

128. Do you and your team notice the behavioural needs of your customer when on the phone? i.e. Do you change your approach to align to the differing behaviours of the customer: happy, calm, serious, etc.

Ask questions

Consider these throughout your customer experience:

129. Do you and your team ask questions to gather information so you can instantly offer the appropriate assistance to your customers when they enter your business? e.g. How may I help you? What brings you to (name of the business) today?

130. Do you and your team ask questions to gather information so you can instantly offer the appropriate assistance to your customers when they phone your business? e.g. How may I help you?

131. Do you and your team ask questions during the customer's experience within your business to establish if they want or need any additional support, information, or service?

132. Do you and your team ask questions to gain further information from your customers, to ensure customers get all they may want and need? Ensuring the best experience possible.

133. Do you and your team ask questions during the customers' time in your business to gather information with the intention of establishing if they are satisfied with their experience so far, so appropriate adjustments can be made to make their experience exceptional?

134. Do you and your team ask your customers their level of satisfaction as they are about to leave your business?

135. Do you and your team ask your customer questions to understand how you could have made their experience even better?

Listen

Consider these throughout your customer experience:

136. Do you and your team show active listening skills when interacting with customers and each other? i.e. stop what you are doing, look at the other person and seem genuinely interested in what is being said and wait for them to finish before making any comment.

137. Do you and your team reflect back your understanding to ensure you have heard the right information to assist your customers?

138. Are you and your team totally focused on the caller when on the phone? i.e. not distracted by looking at computer screens or any other distractions.

139. Do you and your team listen intently whilst on the phone with your customers? Ensuring you are focused entirely on the customer.

Respond

Consider these throughout your customer experience:

140. Do you and your team respond positively to the information received from your customers? e.g. say 'Certainly', 'Yes, of course I shall get this for you now.' 'Let me check this for you.'

141. Do you and your team show positive body language in response to the information you receive from customers? e.g. smile, or with a sense of urgency.

142. Do you and your team respond with what is possible to assist your customers? Giving them options and honest information.

143. Do you and your team respond using language that will be understood by all customers? i.e. free from expert terminology or jargon that might not be understood by others.

144. Do you and your team respond positively, making realistic commitments to your customers?

145. Do you and your team respond positively to your customers' requests when on the phone?

146. Do you and your team have professional body language and a tone of voice that demonstrates that you are attentive when speaking with your customers?

Make it memorable

Consider these throughout your customer experience:

147. Do you and your team actively seek opportunities to create a memorable experience for your customers?

148. Do you and your team make a personal connection with your customers?

149. Do you and your team ensure your customers leave your business with a genuine and personalised farewell?

150. Do you and your team naturally use the customer's name when you know it?

151. Do you and your team work together to share any information you have learned about the customer so this can be used throughout other areas of the customer experience?

152. Do you and your team use conversation to gather more information from your customers so you can make use of this information in order to make it memorable? e.g. special occasions, planned holidays, the well-being of their relative, etc.

153. Do you and your team use conversation to gather the maximum amount of information from your customers on the phone so you can share this with the rest of your team to make their experience memorable?

When you have assessed your business against the 153 standards, then calculate your results as a percentage. This will then give you an annual result which you can compare to your results in the next year, and each year thereafter, no matter how many standards you have. Giving you an opportunity to challenge your own service performance.

APPENDIX B

The Service Standards Checklist template

SERVICE STANDARDS CHECKLIST	YES/ NO
1	
What did you observe/notice?	
2	
What did you observe/notice?	
3	
What did you observe/notice?	
4	
What did you observe/notice?	
5	
What did you observe/notice?	
6	
What did you observe/notice?	

SERVICE STANDARDS CHECKLIST		YES/ NO
7	What did you observe/notice?	
8	What did you observe/notice?	
9	What did you observe/notice?	
10	What did you observe/notice?	
Total: **Comments/What have you learned?**		

APPENDIX C

Sample Service Standards Checklist One:

This is an example of a checklist that was used by an office-based client for the first three months. It is advisable to use each checklist for up to three months to ensure that the standards are embedded within the team.

SERVICE STANDARDS CHECKLIST		YES/ NO
1	When your customers arrive into your business, do they see gleaming, clean windows with no dust, streaks, smears, handprints or water marks on them? *(See)*	
	What did you observe/notice?	
2	Do your customers see colleagues giving instant warm eye contact, standing straight and showing caring body language towards them? *(See and Be there)*	
	What did you observe/notice?	
3	Do your customers hear positive background noise, free from unwanted banging doors, clattering of operational activity not wanted to be heard by the customer? Free from maintenance or engineering noise. *(Hear)*	
	What did you observe/notice?	
4	Do your customers hear your colleagues engaging in friendly and appropriate conversation with them and other customers? *(Hear)*	
	What did you observe/notice?	
5	Are your premises fresh and thoroughly aired? *(Smell)*	
	What did you observe/notice?	

SERVICE STANDARDS CHECKLIST		YES/ NO
6	**Do you and your team have fresh breath?** *(Smell)*	
	What did you observe/notice?	
7	**Does the food you sell look tasty?** *(See and Taste)*	
8	**Do you have high food and drink hygiene scores that you are proud of?** *(See and Taste)*	
	What did you observe/notice?	
9	**Do your customers feel clean, polished surfaces?** *(Feel)*	
	What did you observe/notice?	
10	**Do you and your team greet and acknowledge your customer as they move around in your business or premises?** *(Be there)*	
	What did you observe/notice?	
Total:		
Comments/What have you learned?		

Sample Service Standards Checklist Two:

When you have scored 9 or 10 out of 10 consistently from Checklist One, progress to the next checklist, Checklist Two. Here's an example of a second checklist for the same office-based company as they progressed to incorporate the 6 Steps to Be Exceptional. It is advisable to use each checklist for up to three months to ensure that the standards are embedded within the team.

SERVICE STANDARDS CHECKLIST		YES/ NO
1	Do your customers see the information they want and need on immaculate materials? That is free from creases, debris, graffiti, rips? *(See)*	
	What did you observe/notice?	
2	Do your customers see positive interactions with other customers? Are all colleagues being helpful to all customers? *(See and Be there)*	
	What did you observe/notice?	
3	Do your customers see clean and inviting toilet facilities? That are sparkling clean and free from stains and excessive water around the sinks? *(See and Feel)*	
	What did you observe/notice?	
4	Do your customers hear a genuine warm welcome for themselves and to all other customers? *(Hear)*	
	What did you observe/notice?	
5	Do your customers hear your colleagues engaging in friendly and appropriate conversation with them and other customers? *(Hear and Ask questions)*	
	What did you observe/notice?	

SERVICE STANDARDS CHECKLIST		YES/ NO
6	**Do you and your team wear subtle and understated deodorants, perfume or aftershave which is not overpowering?** *(Smell)*	
	What did you observe/notice?	
7	**Is the food and drink served consistently fresh and tasting good?** *(Taste)*	
	What did you observe/notice?	
8	**Do your customers feel the temperature is at the right level for their comfort?** *(Feel)*	
	What did you observe/notice?	
9	**Do you and your team seem to genuinely want to look after your customers?** *(Be there)*	
	What did you observe/notice?	
10	**Do you and your team communicate with your customers in a caring tone of voice?** *(Watch the signals and Ask questions and Respond)*	
	What did you observe/notice?	
Total:		
Comments/What have you learned?		

Sample Service Standards Checklist Three:

When you have scored 9 or 10 out of 10 consistently from Checklist Two, progress to the next checklist, Checklist Three. This is an example of a checklist used by the same office-based business. It is advisable to use each checklist for up to three months to ensure that the standards are embedded within the team.

SERVICE STANDARDS CHECKLIST		YES/ NO
1	Do your customers hear all colleagues greeting them throughout the whole of the business? *(Hear and Be there)*	
	What did you observe/notice?	
2	Do your customers see all colleagues giving your undivided attention to the customer they are interacting with? Listening careful and responding appropriately? *(See, Be there, Listen and Respond)*	
	What did you observe/notice?	
3	Do your customers hear clear and succinct information they need to be aware of, in a way they understand? *(Hear and Respond)*	
	What did you observe/notice?	
4	Are your premises free from any musty, mould or stale food smells? *(Smell)*	
	What did you observe/notice?	
5	Are you and your team looking up in anticipation for customers arriving into your business or your area of the business? *(See and Be there)*	
	What did you observe/notice?	

SERVICE STANDARDS CHECKLIST	YES/ NO
6 Do you and your team ask how their experience was? With the intention of learning from that customer experience and gaining information to potentially improve for the future? *(Ask questions and Respond)*	
What did you observe/notice?	
7 Do you and your team ask questions to gather information so you can instantly offer the appropriate assistance to your customers when they enter your business? e.g. How may I help you? What brings you to (name of the business) today? *(Be there, Ask questions, Listen, Respond and Make it memorable)*	
What did you observe/notice?	
8 Do you and your team show active listening skills when interacting with customers and each other? i.e. stop what you're doing, look at the other person and seem genuinely interested in what is being said and wait for them to finish before making any comment. *(Listen)*	
What did you observe/notice?	
9 Do you and your team show positive body language in response to the information you receive from your customers? e.g. smile, or with a sense of urgency *(Respond)*	
What did you observe/notice?	
10 Do you and your team offer a genuine 'farewell' to your customers? With a message along the lines of 'We look forward to seeing you again.' *(Be there and Make it memorable)*	
What did you observe/notice?	
Total: **Comments/What have you learned?**	

Sample Service Standards Checklist Four:

When you have scored 9 or 10 out of 10 consistently from Checklist Three, progress to the next checklist, Checklist Four. This is an example used by the same office-based business. To maintain a focus on service, as well as continuing to monitor the checklist daily/weekly, you should also review its relevance to the needs of your business and make any necessary changes every quarter.

SERVICE STANDARDS CHECKLIST		YES/ NO
1	**Do your customers see all colleagues prioritising the customer before tasks and their colleagues?** *(See and Be there)*	
	What did you observe/notice?	
2	**Do your customers hear your colleagues explore solutions to their needs?** *(Hear, Ask questions, Listen and Respond)*	
	What did you observe/notice?	
3	**Do your customers hear what the colleague had understood from the customers' expectations?** *(Hear and Listen)*	
	What did you observe/notice?	
4	**Do your customers smell aromas that complement the surroundings?** *(Smell)*	
	What did you observe/notice?	
5	**Are you and your team present as the customer needs additional assistance?** *(Be there)*	
	What did you observe/notice?	

SERVICE STANDARDS CHECKLIST	YES/ NO
6 Do you and your team switch your behaviour to meet the needs of the customer? i.e. When the customer is looking happy, the colleague welcomes them positively. If they look concerned or serious, does the colleague welcome them in a calm tone. *(Watch the signals)* What did you observe/notice?	
7 Do you and your team ask questions during the customer's time in your business to gather information to establish if they are satisfied with their experiences so far, so you make the appropriate adjustments to make their experience exceptional? *(Ask, Listen, Respond and Make it memorable)* What did you observe/notice?	
8 Do you and your team reflect back your understanding to ensure you have heard the right information to assist your customers? *(Listen)* What did you observe/notice?	
9 Do you and your team respond positively to the information received from your customer? e.g. say 'Certainly', 'Yes, of course, I shall get this for you now', 'Let me check this for you.' *(Respond)* What did you observe/notice?	
10 Do you and your team use conversation to gather more information from your customers so you can make use of this information in order to make it memorable? e.g. special occasions, planned holidays, the well-being of their relatives, etc. *(Ask questions, Listen, Respond and Make it memorable)* What did you observe/notice?	
Total: **Comments/What have you learned?**	

Here's an example of a Service Standards Checklist for Phone Use:

When you have scored 9 or 10 out of 10 consistently from Checklist Three, progress to the next checklist, Checklist Four. This is an example used by the same office-based business. To maintain a focus on service, as well as continuing to monitor the checklist daily/weekly, you should also review its relevance to the needs of your business and make any necessary changes every quarter.

	SERVICE STANDARDS CHECKLIST	YES/ NO
1	**Do you and your team answer the phone within 3 rings?** *(Be there)*	
	What did you observe/notice?	
2	**Do your customers hear your colleagues engaging in friendly and appropriate conversation?** *(Hear)*	
	What did you observe/notice?	
3	**Do your customers hear full sentences that make sense?** *(Hear and Ask questions)*	
	What did you observe/notice?	
4	**Do your customers hear clear and succinct information they need to be aware of, in a way they understand?** *(Hear and Respond)*	
	What did you observe/notice?	
5	**Do you and your team communicate calmly and with confidence with your customers?** *(Hear and Respond)*	
	What did you observe/notice?	

SERVICE STANDARDS CHECKLIST		YES/ NO
6	**Do you and your team communicate with your customers in a caring tone of voice?** *(Hear, Be there, Watch the signals and Respond)*	
	What did you observe/notice?	
7	**Do you and your team use conversation to gather the maximum amount of information from your customers on the phone so you can share this with the rest of your team to make their experience memorable?** *(Hear and Ask questions)*	
	What did you observe/notice?	
8	**Do you and your team listen intently whist on the phone with your customers? Ensuring you are focused entirely on the customer.** *(Listen and Respond)*	
	What did you observe/notice?	
9	**Do you and your team respond positively to your customers' requests when on the phone?** *(Hear, Listen and Respond)*	
	What did you observe/notice?	
10	**Do you and your team offer a genuine 'farewell' to your customers?** *(Hear, Respond and Make it memorable)*	
	What did you observe/notice?	
Total:		
Comments/What have you learned?